At Table With Jesus

John O. Gooch

ABINGDON PRESS
Nashville

AT TABLE WITH JESUS

by John O. Gooch

ISBN 978-0-687-09075-4

MANUFACTURED IN THE UNITED STATES OF AMERICA

07 08 09 10 11—10 9 8 7 6 5 4 3

Contents

Meet the Writer

John O. Gooch is a native Missourian who has recently returned home, "where the air is just better." He is a husband, father, grandfather, brother, cousin, friend. One of his great joys in the past year has been "reconnecting" with cousins across the US and enjoying meals and conversation with them.

John is a graduate of Central Methodist College (1956), Garrett/Evangelical Theological Seminary (1963), and received the Ph.D. in historical theology from St. Louis University in 1983. He is a clergy member of the Missouri East Conference, where he pastored churches for twenty-three years. In addition, he has been an editor at The United Methodist Publishing House, a free-lance writer, and a youth ministry consultant and trainer.

John and his wife, Beth, have two children and two grandchildren. John's passions are church history and youth ministry. His hobbies include genealogy, travel, camping, hiking, and eating lunch with friends.

A Word of Welcome

Welcome to this study of AT TABLE WITH JESUS. Jesus said and did so many things in his brief earthly sojourn that he could have been remembered in many ways by his disciples. This resource will help you discover why Jesus commanded that he be remembered in the breaking of bread and why the church continues to celebrate the risen Christ by gathering around the table. In infinite wisdom God ordained that the Son should reveal the very heart of God through the meals he shared with others.

In this study you will explore

- Jesus creating fellowship as guest rather than as host;
- Jesus eating with anyone who welcomed him;
- Jesus celebrating feasts rather than observing fasts;
- Jesus satisfying the hunger of all;
- Jesus at table as witness to the heavenly banquet in the kingdom of God.

The power of Jesus' table fellowship is not found in the miraculous or supernatural; rather, we see the divine made present in the daily, ordinary mealtime. At table, Jesus revealed that we can depend on our heavenly Father to provide our daily bread and that we can live in thankfulness for all God's gifts. The simple life of trusting God to provide for us, humbly accepting the gifts of the earth, sharing God's gifts with all in need, and expressing gratitude is the essential shape of Christian discipleship. When we are faithful to Christ's command to remember him at table, he keeps his promise and becomes our guest. So, welcome Christ as your guest as you engage your heart and mind to reflect on God's revelation seen in Jesus' table fellowship.

How to Use This Resource

We hope you enjoy participating in this study, either on your own or with a group. We offer these hints and suggestions to make your study a success.

At Table With Jesus is a self-contained study with all the teaching/learning suggestions conveniently located on or near the main text to which they refer. They are identified with the same heading (or a close abbreviation) as the heading in the main text. In addition to your Bible, all you need to have a successful group or individual study session is provided for you in this book.

Some special features are provided as well, such as the **Bible 301** activities in the teaching helps. We usually think of the "101" designation as the beginning level; these "301" designations prompt you to dig deeper. In these instances you will be invited to look up Scriptures, key words, or concepts in a Bible dictionary, commentary, or atlas. On occasion, an added book or resource is cited that may be obtained from your local library or perhaps from your pastor. Those resources are extras; your study will be enriched by these added sources of information, but it is not dependent on them.

This study is intentionally invitational. In the closing activity, you are invited to do three things: to give prayerful consideration to your relationship to Jesus Christ and make or renew your commitment, to offer your own spoken prayers, and to pray with and for others. We trust you will participate in these activities as you feel comfortable and that you will use them as a challenge to grow more confident with prayer and with your covenant with Jesus Christ.

Be Legal

Several suggestions are given for showing a videocassette to your group (see pages 19, 20, 41, 46). Be aware of the legal restrictions involved.

The Copyright Act grants to the copyright owner the exclusive right, among others, "to perform the copyrighted work publicly" (Section 106).

The rental or purchase of a home videocassette does not carry with it the right "to perform the copyrighted work publicly" (Section 202). *Publicly* means outside a home in "a normal circle of family and its social acquaintances" (Section 101).

Home videocassettes may be shown, without a license, in certain narrowly defined "face-to-face teaching activities," in a setting "devoted to instruction" (Section 110.1), because the law makes a specific, limited exception for such showing. *There are no other exceptions.*

Your church or conference may be covered by a site license for public performance for video. If not, contact The Motion Picture Licensing Corporation's Church Desk (800-515-8855). All nonhome use of videos available in video stores requires a license.

Session One

Practicing Hospitality

Session Focus ■

This session focuses on table fellowship, an important virtue, one that can create community and intimacy in our relationships.

Session Objective ■

You will explore table fellowship and see how it can become a mark of true discipleship.

Session Preparation ■

Think about the part that hospitality/meals play in your life. Would you rather eat alone or with friends? What do you experience around the table at family gatherings? What changes would you like to make in your life that relate to hospitality?

Choose from among these activities and discussion starters to plan your lesson.

Practicing Hospitality ■

Ask: What do people do in restaurants when they eat alone? If you are doing this study as part of a group,

I was on a business trip and alone in a different city. Maybe that's why I was so aware of other people in the restaurant. Some were eating together in small groups. Other tables were shared by couples. Many were like me—alone. There is a strange kind of sadness about people eating by themselves. They stare off into space and try not to make eye contact with anyone. Or they hide behind a book or a newspaper. (I always take a book with me when I eat alone.) People feel exposed and vulnerable when they eat alone. Maybe that's how Matthew or Zacchaeus felt at the end of the day, when they left their tax-gathering booths. No wonder they were so eager to share a meal with Jesus!

The New Testament church never considered eating alone. Table fellowship was a key part of the common life. Eating together reminded them of the coming of Jesus and the breaking in of the kingdom of God. When they "remembered Jesus," they remembered that he had gone out to those whom polite society scorned and invited himself to their tables. At those tables, the grace of God, the Kingdom itself, broke in, in new and powerful ways. So eating together was important to the early church not just for the food and fellowship, but for the remembrance.

The Jerusalem church, as reflected in the

tell each other stories about eating alone in a strange place, in a strange town. What do you do when you eat alone? Do you want to have a book or a newspaper with you? Can that "protection" also be a way to shut others out, so they won't bother you?

Hospitality as a Virtue ■

Read Psalm 23:5-6 and Genesis 18:1-8. In what specific ways do those verses show examples of table fellowship? What do they suggest about table fellowship as a virtue? Do you see in both of them some of the rules of hospitality outlined in this chapter?

Book of Acts, ate their meals together "with glad and generous hearts" (Acts 2:46). Paul fought with Peter and the followers of James over the question of Christians being free to eat together in Antioch (see Session Two) and upbraided the Corinthian church because they were not being open and hospitable about their common meals. Table fellowship is a radical thing that the Christian church brought into the pagan world.

In this session, we will look first at hospitality as the background for table fellowship, then at three stories from the life of Jesus that illustrate the life-giving and life-receiving fellowship to be found at table.

Hospitality as a Virtue

In the nomadic world of Israel's ancestors, hospitality was a cardinal virtue. It may have been practiced partly out of fear, but it was certainly practiced. When the three strangers came to visit Abraham and Sarah (Genesis 18), Abraham suggested a little lunch—which turned out to be an entire roast calf and enough bread to feed far more than the three strangers. He brought water for them to wash and stopped whatever he was doing to talk with them and make them welcome. Ancient custom also decreed that, if you were a stranger and a Bedouin took you into his tent and fed you (gave you bread and salt), you were under his protection while you were with him and for a designated period after you left his tent. This union of hospitality and safety is reflected in the last part of Psalm 23, where a table is prepared "in the presence of" the psalmist's enemies. The anointing of the head and the overflowing cup are signs of a gracious and generous host.

In the New Testament, the Greek word

"No one is a stranger, except in relationship to someone else." What do you think that means? Why do we call *xenophobia* one of the great sins of our time? What are some specific examples you may have seen in the news recently? (Hint: Rejection of migrant workers, resentment against Asians and other immigrants.)

not just the foreigner

Notice that the Greek word for hospitality occurs in *xenophobia*. What does that mean to you in terms of our relationships with other people? If we think of hospitality as a way of making strangers into friends, how would we do that with homeless persons on the street? What about the stranger who visits our church?

xenos means "stranger," but also "guest" or "host." This suggests a powerful truth—that no one is a stranger except in relationship to someone else. That is, we make one another strangers or guests depending on how we treat one another. From this Greek word comes the description of one of the great sins of our time: *xenophobia*, or fear of the stranger. You see that word in action every time you walk down a city street. People look right through you (particularly if you appear to be poor or homeless). Doors are locked; some windows have bars; requests for help, even directions, are routinely ignored. We "don't want to get involved." We need to protect ourselves.

In that light it is interesting that the New Testament word for hospitality, *philoxenia*, comes from the same root. It means love of the guest or the stranger. It can mean a love of the whole atmosphere of hospitality, of guesting and hosting. Isn't it fascinating how close love of the stranger and fear of the stranger come to each other?

Hospitality is, by its very nature, hard work. It takes place under risky conditions. When we welcome a stranger, we never know what might happen. Even in "safe" circumstances, we always wonder if we will like the person, if he or she will like us, or if the time we spend together be fascinating or dreadfully boring. In other circumstances, we run a risk when we stop to help a stranded traveler or offer assistance to a homeless person asking for food. And there is no structure for welcoming strangers. That is, there are no easy steps through which we go to be hospitable. Every encounter brings a new set of challenges and opportunities. Often, many of us allow fear to crowd out what needs to be done in hospitality.

Bethea's in Kenya

Jesus did something even more risky—he moved beyond inviting persons to eat with him and went to eat with them. For example, he didn't say to Zacchaeus, "come down and let's go to lunch." He said, "I'm eating at your house today." So what does that mean for us? It reminds us that God brings God's agenda into the midst of our world. Beyond all the normal rules for hospitality, God's prevenient grace seeks out those who are lost and alone and brings them into fellowship. Jesus was known in his world as one who ate with sinners and got into all kinds of trouble for it. But he was bringing a radical new dimension to table fellowship. The kingdom of God was coming to reality in these meals.

Word ?—
Before
coming?

Mary and Martha: Luke 10:38-42

Mary and Martha
Read Luke 10:38-42. What two kinds of hospitality do you see in this story? How many social "rules" do you see broken? What social barriers have you seen broken down in your lifetime? How were they broken?

"Debate" Mary and Martha. What is hospitality for each of them? What arguments could be put forth to support Martha's position about hospitality? to support Mary's? Think carefully: did Jesus ever deny that Martha had a point?

This delightful story concerns at least two kinds of hospitality—and a wide range of rules that are broken by Jesus and the two sisters. In first-century Jewish culture, it was considered highly improper for a rabbi, such as Jesus, to be seen in public alone with a woman. Think of all the moral and social barriers through which Jesus went crashing when he accepted an invitation to Martha's home—apparently without even considering appearances.

Mary then proceeded to break more social rules. It was not proper etiquette for women to listen to the teaching of a rabbi as if she were a disciple. What does this mean? In the first place, she would be neglecting her responsibility as a member of the household. She should have been helping Martha with the meal. By sitting at Jesus' feet, she was acting like a male. This was a violation of a clear social boundary, and she was bringing shame upon her house. Yet here she was, oblivious to all the social consequences, sitting at Jesus' feet, drinking in his every word. There is nothing ordinary about this story!

Martha was concerned with hospitality. She wanted to be a good hostess, so she immediately began preparing a meal. We need to take a good look at what Martha was doing here, for she often gets "bad press" about this situation. It's too easy to say she should have stopped what she was doing and listened to Jesus. Unlike Mary, she was staying in her proper social role and bringing no shame on her house. Unlike Mary, she was living up to the traditions and expectations of hospitality. She was being the perfect hostess. By her own standards, she was doing exactly what she should have been doing.

For Mary, on the other hand, hospitality was more than food and drink. It involved being willing to listen to Jesus, being quiet enough so she could receive what he had to offer. Hospitality can mean listening, as well as feeding!

Martha tried to get things back on the proper track, by suggesting that Jesus tell Mary to get up and help. Jesus gently reminded Martha there is more to hospitality than a good meal—there is also the living Word. Hospitality means being sensitive to the needs of the guest, as well as to the rules of society.

Dolly madison & the finger bowls

The first time we ever entertained a bishop in our home, we made elaborate preparations, even knowing it would be well into the evening when he arrived. When the time finally came, he was more than willing to eat a sandwich (he'd missed his dinner); but what he really wanted was to get his shoes off and find out if the Cardinals had defeated the Yankees that afternoon! As Saint Augustine said somewhere in a sermon, "Martha is what we are; Mary is what we hope to become."

The Sending of the Seventy ■

Read Luke 10:1-12. Why would we include this passage in a discussion of hospitality?

The Sending of the Seventy: Luke 10:1-12

This passage is a story about evangelism—about sending out seventy disciples to spread the word of the coming Kingdom through Galilee. In the process of instructing the evangelists, Jesus also told them (and us) a great deal about how to receive hospitality. Hospitality in this story is about taking the good news to those who have not heard it—and, in return, accepting their hospitality. In the words of the disciples, the Kingdom was breaking in—and people were responding to it with openness and hospitality.

First, when the disciples entered a house, they were to say, "Peace to this house!" Then they were to stay where they were received. No matter what kind of temptation "better" offers might bring, they were to stay with the house where they were first offered hospitality. Implicit in these sayings is the understanding that the character of the *host* is revealed by how he receives the disciples and their message.

Receiving hospitality is as important as giving it—and perhaps more difficult. We once had an overnight guest whom I invited home from a meeting so he wouldn't have to stay in an impersonal motel. The next day, he complained about the showerhead, about what I served for breakfast, and several other things. He was, to say the least, *not* a gracious guest.

Second, the host provides hospitality, food, and drink. When the host and the disciples eat and drink together, they implicitly do away with all social barriers. There are no longer any differences of wealth, or class, or power, or race. They are simply brothers and sisters in Christ.

Third, there are some explicit directions

Why is *receiving* hospitality so important? Why do you think many would rather give hospitality (or a gift) than receive it?

One of the most popular slogans of our day is WWJD?—"What Would Jesus Do?" Think about two or three situations in your church and/or community where social barriers have meant persons were not welcomed or accepted.

For each of those situations, what would Jesus do? (And the corollary, if that's what Jesus would do, what would Jesus expect his disciples to do?)

Think about building community. What does the story about the author's experience as a guest in the church suggest about community? When we eat with others, what happens between us?

Bible 301 ☐

Explore ways your congregation can offer table fellowship to others in the community, perhaps through the Room in the Inn program or other service ministries in your community.

What is the relationship between mission and hospitality? OR, If there are homeless persons in your community, or persons who are hungry, what is the relationship between mission and hospitality? What would Jesus expect his disciples to do about those situations?

for the mission of the seventy that tell us a great deal both about hospitality and the building up of community. The disciples were to eat what was provided—and the community would be created through table fellowship. I was once a workshop leader in a church where there were several adults who had severe mental disabilities. As the guest, I was asked to go through the buffet line first. I found a table and sat down with my plate— and discovered that the next person to sit down was one of the mentally disabled adults. The other adults in the congregation did not sit down with us. So he and I ate our meal together in silence, except for the mewing sounds that he made from time to time. Later, I discovered that, even though his sitting there had been accidental, it was a test of how hospitable I was; how willing was I to share myself with a member of their community? Our sense of community in that congregation was built through this act of table fellowship.

The disciples were to heal the sick, that is, to care for the physical needs of the persons with whom they came in contact. Dealing with hunger, sickness, pain, disability are all signs of hospitality. Indeed, in Matthew 25, Jesus suggests that the ultimate test of hospitality is what we do about physical needs. When we feed the hungry, clothe the naked, visit the prisoner, we offer hospitality not only to them, but to Jesus himself.

Finally, the disciples are called to announce the Kingdom, to proclaim the good news. In a similar fashion, we find the words of Jesus in Revelation 3:20, "Listen! I am standing at the door, knocking; if you hear my voice and open the door, I will come in to you and eat with you, and you with me." This was said to those who, by becoming lukewarm in the faith, had effectively shut the door against Jesus. Yet Jesus invited himself into their lives. Inviting himself into their lives was announcing the good news of the Kingdom.

Jesus and the Harlot ▪

Read Luke 7:36-50. Outline the plot of the story. List each event in proper sequence. With each event, note the violation of social conventions. What were all the social conventions that were violated by the woman and Jesus?

Jesus and the Harlot: Luke 7:36-50

A certain Pharisee gave a banquet. Both Jesus and a woman came to the banquet, but only one of them had been invited. In the Palestine of Jesus' day, it was customary to have banquets out-of-doors, so the poor of the community could watch. In one way, this was like television—a mindless sort of entertainment when you had nothing better to do. In another way, it was an act of hospitality of sorts—the poor were often invited to eat the food that was left. This story happened in Galilee, according to Luke, early in Jesus' ministry. It has no apparent connection to similar stories in the Gospels about the woman anointing Jesus before his burial.

Did you ever wonder about how this woman actually anointed Jesus' feet? I used to have these mental pictures of her somehow crawling under the table so she could get to Jesus' feet. (And then what did she do about his shoes and socks?) Or else Jesus was extremely cooperative and turned his chair so she could easily reach his feet. Then I discovered something about social customs of the day. Diners reclined on couches that were placed at an angle to the table. They leaned on their left elbows and ate with their right hands. Their feet hung off the end of the short couch—*and*, I learned, it was the custom to take off their sandals at the door and a house slave brought them water and washed the dust off their feet before they went in! In this case, the host neglected this basic act of hospitality.

The woman's act expressed love and gratitude—but it also violated social conventions.
(People around Jesus were always violating
social conventions. But, then, so was Jesus.)
Touching or caressing a man's feet possesses
intimate overtones. So did letting down her
hair. For any woman to have done this would
have been socially explosive. Additionally,
this woman was a known prostitute and,
therefore, ritually unclean. For her to touch
Jesus in any way made him ritually unclean
as well. The woman's act and Jesus' acceptance of it bordered on the scandalous.

The Pharisee, Simon, was properly scandalized. The woman was an affront to his
honor and to that of Jesus. In considering
how to deal with the situation, the Pharisee
made two assumptions:

1. The woman is a sinner.
2. If Jesus were a prophet, he would know
   what sort of woman she is.

Both assumptions were, in fact, correct. So
far, Simon was doing fine. But then he proceeded to make two false deductions from
his correct assumptions. First, he deduced
that, if Jesus knew what sort of woman was
touching him, he would not allow it. But
Jesus did know; and he did allow her to
touch him, for reasons that had nothing to
do with social convention, sexuality, or ritual
purity. Second, Simon deduced that, since
Jesus did nothing to stop the woman, he was
not a prophet. Again, Simon was wrong.
Jesus not only knew what kind of woman she
was, he knew what kind of man Simon was,
too.

It was common at banquets for the host
and the guests to pose riddles for each other
in a kind of friendly contest of wit and wisdom. That custom is reflected in verses 40-
47. Jesus told a story about two debtors and

How did Jesus "set Simon
up" with his riddle? What
is the relationship of the
riddle to hospitality?

asked Simon which will be more grateful for having the debt forgiven. The scale of the two debts was relatively modest, but well beyond the means of any but the very wealthy. A denarius was an average day's wage for a working man, so 500 denarii would be nearly two years wages. The answer to the riddle was obvious, and Simon gave the answer in a kind of flippant tone that suggested, "Come on, that's no riddle. You can do better than this." But his answer sprung the trap!

Jesus confirmed that Simon gave the right answer. Then Jesus drew a parallel between his obvious riddle and what happened at the meal. Simon had not been hospitable at all, and the woman had been incredibly generous. Simon did not give Jesus any of the forms of hospitality—no water for the feet, no kiss of greeting, no oil of anointing for the head. In contrast, the woman washed his feet with her tears and dried them with her hair. She kissed his feet and anointed them with ointment.

Verse 47 is the point of the story. Because she had many sins (a great debt) that had been forgiven, she was responding with great love. Simon, on the other hand, did not even recognize he needed to be forgiven; so he received very little. The riddle had come back around and bitten Simon from behind! This is the powerful sign of the breaking in of the kingdom of God. Sins are forgiven. The outcast are welcomed into fellowship. Love breaks down barriers. And those who have responded to the Kingdom offer acts of love and hospitality in return.

Close With Prayer

Close with this prayer:

Gracious God, you give us so much more than we deserve. And you set an example for us that stretches our willingness to serve you. Help us learn how to become gracious hosts, so we can give hospitality and how to become gracious recipients of hospitality. Help us see hospitality is something that goes beyond lunches, dinners, and parties, but is an attitude that embraces all of life; in the name of Jesus Christ. Amen.

Session Two

Eating With Sinners

Session Focus ■

This session focuses on Jesus' words and examples of hospitality and how he expected his disciples to be open.

Session Objective ■

You will discover how Jesus defied the social and religious mores of his day in order to invite those who had been driven to the margins of society into God's kingdom. You will also learn that Jesus calls us to act in open, inclusive, inviting ways.

Session Preparation ■

You will need a Bible dictionary, a copy of the video, *Jesus of Nazareth,* and a VCR. **See pages 6–7 for information about legally showing videos to a group. Copyright laws are strict.**

Choose from among these activities and discussion starters to plan your lesson.

Jesus was forever in trouble with some members of the religious establishment, primarily because he couldn't observe some of their rules and regulations—not when people's lives were at stake. He was notorious for "eating with sinners." In fact, he was called a drunkard and a glutton (Matthew 11:19), because he was so often at dinner parties, usually with people who were outside the acceptable orders of society. In this chapter, we will look at two stories that report Jesus ate with tax collectors. These stories raise questions about the meaning of table fellowship. Then we will look at a story about table fellowship in the New Testament church that will help us see some directions for applying Jesus' actions and teachings to our own lives and congregations.

The Call of Matthew: Matthew 9:9-13; Mark 2:13-17; Luke 5:27-32

"Jesus didn't come for us." With those attention-grabbing words, Bishop Eugene Frank began a sermon to the Missouri East Annual Conference, some thirty-five years ago. After he had our attention, he declared that Jesus came for sinners, not for the righteous. Those who consider themselves righteous and aren't willing to listen to what Jesus says, or to be open to Jesus' hospitality to those "in need of a physician," are somehow left out of the Kingdom. "Sinners," on the

Begin by watching a segment from the video, *Jesus of Nazareth*. The segment includes the call of Matthew and then a dinner party that Matthew threw for his (sinner) friends and Jesus.

Tell the group to watch for signs of hospitality (Peter and the other disciples watching from the doorway, for example) and how the disciples reacted to the party. Continue watching through the scene on the beach where Peter is angry about how easy it was for Matthew to "get in." What does this segment say to us about hospitality in Jesus' day? about the way Peter felt? as an example for how we might feel?

The Call of Matthew ■

Read Matthew 9:9-13 and the parallels in Mark and Luke. Compare the three accounts. Are there any significant differences? If so, what? Call attention to what this chapter says about "toll collectors," how they made their money and how society felt about them.

other hand, listen to his words and are open to the hospitality that he offers. That seems to be one point behind the stories of the call of the tax collector (Levi/Matthew).

First, let's clear up some minor points. What was the name of this tax collector? Matthew calls him *Matthew*, Luke calls him *Levi*, and Mark calls him *Levi son of Alphaeus*. In the various lists of Jesus' disciples there is a *James, son of Alphaeus*, but no Levi. Although there may be a lack of clarity regarding the identity of the tax collector, this minor detail does not change the point of the story; the story is still about hospitality to sinners. In this chapter, we will continue to call the tax collector "Matthew," since that is the more common usage.

The other "minor" point is what Matthew did. He was not like an agent of our Internal Revenue Service, checking over our tax returns to be sure we pay our full share. "Customs collector" is probably a more accurate description of what he did as a "tax collector." He collected customs on goods crossing the border into Herod Antipas's domain, probably with headquarters in Capernaum, which was the nearest city to the border. To get the job in the first place, Matthew had contracted with the authorities to deliver a certain amount of money each year from the customs. That done, he could set the customs fees at whatever level he wanted. So long as he met his contracted minimum, the authorities did not particularly care how much he charged for personal gain. The potential for corruption and for gaining great wealth at the expense of merchants is obvious. Customs collectors were highly unpopular. *Sinner* expresses something of the social contempt in which they were held. Actually, there was no law against eating with customs collectors; nevertheless, the Pharisees would always abstain. In fact, the strictest Pharisees ate only with other Pharisees so as to avoid ritual impurity.

Jesus and Matthew ■

"People are not lining up to become disciples." Why, do you think, is that so? Why do you think Jesus called Matthew? How is it a "sign of hope and joy" that Jesus called Matthew?

Jesus and the Call of Matthew

This story shows first of all that Jesus' call was effective. People were not lining up to volunteer to become disciples—of Jesus, or anyone else. But Jesus called persons (Peter, Andrew, the sons of Zebedee, Matthew) and they left everything and followed him. Whom did Jesus call? Not those who were "worthy." He rejected those who thought they could become disciples and called those who were rejected by society. Matthew had no apparent qualifications for being a disciple. He was a social pariah, considered a traitor because he worked for an occupying power (Rome) and certainly did not comply with Jewish religious traditions. But think about this—if Jesus could call Matthew, he could call anyone. For the person who watched and listened to Jesus, this was a sign of hope and joy. If Jesus were willing to call a toll collector, he might even call me! Anyone may be welcome in Jesus' fellowship! That reality remains a sign of hope to the whole world.

What was Jesus' real offense in eating with Matthew and his friends? Whom did he offend? What dinner parties would Jesus have today that would offend us?

It isn't clear who threw the party—Luke says it was Levi; Matthew and Mark are ambiguous. But the power of the party is clear, regardless of confusion about the host. Jesus was clearly the center of the party, though he was not the host. The banquet became a time of joy and celebration. It celebrated that one who was lost had been found, and that the Kingdom was opening up to sinners.

The Gospels were written several decades after Jesus' death and resurrection, so they express both what happened in Jesus' ministry and how the church remembered and celebrated that ministry. Meals were important to the Christian community—Christians defined themselves in terms of the Lord's Supper and of the coming heavenly banquet. They were a community of people who had been called into being through Jesus' death (recalled by the bread and wine of the Supper) and who looked forward to the coming of the Kingdom in all its fullness when they would feast at the heavenly banquet. So meals were an important practice in the life of the church.

With whom one ate was an important issue in the Jewish setting of the Gospels. The Pharisees, as we have seen, observed the laws of ritual purity by eating only with their own kind. Eating with "sinners" brought shame upon Jesus and the early church, because of their blatant refusal to follow the Pharisaic tradition. To the Pharisees, Jesus and the disciples were making themselves ritually unclean by showing that they accepted sinners. The real offense was that Jesus was showing God's radical grace. He did not require people like Matthew to conform to the rules of the Pharisees before he ate with him. Think about that. We are perfectly willing to forgive and accept sinners in the church, but first we want them to reform and become good.

There is something important about the need for repentance. We don't want to get caught in the "cheap grace" trap. But look at Jesus—listen to what he says about God's unconditional love. "Follow me," he said to Matthew; and away they went to a party together. I can even imagine, if Matthew were the host, that he invited his customs collector friends to meet Jesus for themselves. More ritually unclean people; and worse, Jesus hadn't even called them!

> How do we accept persons whom we (and society) consider sinners? What do we expect of "sinners" before we are willing to welcome them?

Eat and Be Blessed ◼

How do you feel on Communion Sunday before the sacrament? after the sacrament?

Bible 301 ☐

Look up publican, Matthew (the disciple), and Zacchaeus in a Bible dictionary. Why were these people considered outcasts in Jewish society? Who are some "publicans" in our society?

What elements seek to define who may come to the Table in the church today? How does the church create its own definitions in distinction to outside forces that seek to set the definition for the church?

Eat and Be Blessed

Think about the biggest party meal in the church's life—Holy Communion. Yet we have people in every congregation who won't receive Communion because they feel unworthy. They miss the point that God loves them unconditionally and that the sacrament is not about worthiness: It's about God's love for all of us, reaching out into our unworthiness.

Actually, none of us is "worthy" on our own merits. We are worthy only because God counts us worthy in the divine invitation lavished upon us. On the other hand, others keep a careful check on persons with whom others eat. As used here, *eat* is a symbol of acceptance in general, not just a description of ingesting food and drink. For pastors or laity to invite "sinners" who have not repented will always draw sharp criticism from some persons in the church.

In the first century, meals like the one in Matthew's home were public. The meal was eaten in the courtyard of the house, and anyone could look in and see what was happening. So the Pharisees watched, and then complained to Jesus' disciples about how the preacher was disgracing himself and the religious community by eating with sinners. This story probably reflects historical reality on two levels: On the first level, it reflects conflicts between Jesus and the Pharisees. On the second level, it reflects conflicts between Matthew's church and the synagogue. The early Jewish-Christian church (which Matthew's almost certainly was) faced continual criticism because it accepted non-Jews in its fellowship.

Jesus' response was that the healthy did not need a physician and that he had come for the sick. It's interesting that this was a common proverb in *Hellenistic* culture, the "worldly" culture of the ancient Roman world. This suggests that Galilee and Galilean carpenters were more involved in a more cosmopolitan, open society than we used to think. Matthew adds to that Hellenistic saying the quotation from Hosea 6:6 about mercy. The point of that quotation in this context seems to be that the mercy of God takes priority over everything else. Everything, including religious tradition, must be understood in the light of God's mercy. That's why Jesus was so open to table fellowship with "sinners."

All three Gospels then add the saying about Jesus coming for sinners, not for the righteous. The common expectation among the religious folk of Jesus' day was that the righteous, those who suffered at the hands of the foreign oppressors or the wicked among their own people, would be saved and those who oppressed them punished. This expectation was, in fact, a common understanding of what salvation would mean. We find this expectation at least as far back in history as the prophet Amos (about 725 B.C.), and it was clearly prevalent in Jesus' day. Jesus set out to redefine the meaning of salvation with this saying.

For Jesus, salvation was not a matter of punishing the sinner; rather, Jesus forgave sin. Jesus sought out those whom society considered evil and accepted their hospitality and all the reciprocal obligations that go with hospitality. The offer of forgiveness and table fellowship was a radical step. It was an intentional move to break down the barriers that divided the "good" from the "sinners." Salvation is a matter of welcoming the sinner, and then "throwing a party" to celebrate that the sinner has come into the Kingdom.

Faithful discipleship is not about separating ourselves from the evil in society.

Jesus said that faithful disciples associate with sinners and invite them into the community of faith. Faithful disciples invite and welcome sinners and offer the love of God in the name of Jesus Christ.

The Call of Zacchaeus ■

Read Luke 19:1-10. Be sure all the plot elements are clear in your mind. Who was Zacchaeus? What was his social dilemma in this story?

The Call of Zacchaeus: Luke 19:1-10

Over the years, I have helped several times with "Room in the Inn," a ministry that provides dinner, a night's lodging, and breakfast for homeless persons in our city. At first, I thought that meeting physical needs was what the ministry was about. Then I discovered that Room in the Inn is about more than food and a place to sleep; it is about table fellowship and hospitality. The real power of the evening is not in serving food, but in sitting at table with homeless men, hearing their stories, and being personally available to them. That was also part of the power of Jesus calling sinners to hospitality, a power that we can see clearly in the story of the call of Zacchaeus.

Zacchaeus was a rich man, a customs collector who made a private fortune out of the power given him by the occupying army. The rich and powerful don't get a "good press" in Luke (see Luke 1:46-55), so we would expect to hear words of judgment on the wealthy here.

In order to see Jesus, Zacchaeus climbed up the tree. This is undignified in itself— grown men don't climb trees, particularly not grown men of Zacchaeus's importance. He wanted to see Jesus. Although we assume Zacchaeus was short in stature, grammatically it is not possible to determine whether Jesus or Zacchaeus was the short person in the story. Imagine how people in the crowd must have nudged each other and laughed out loud at the sight of this hated toll collector climbing up a tree. There was no dignity in that—the man clearly was not "our kind."

How do we see Jesus' table fellowship present in this story? How did Jesus restore dignity and honor to Zacchaeus? What response did Zacchaeus make to Jesus' offer of table fellowship?

Jesus restored dignity and honor to Zacchaeus—again by crossing all the barriers of ritual purity and social contempt. Jesus invited himself to Zacchaeus's home. Hospitality doesn't always mean being the host. Sometimes the most hospitable act is the one where we go to the home of another, in the face of public resistance to our going. Zacchaeus responded to Jesus' hospitality by changing his life. He made amends for his past wrongs, even exceeding the legal demands for restitution. His were the white-collar crimes of fraud and extortion. Jewish law required restitution for such crimes wherever that was possible. The most stringent legal requirement was that Zacchaeus make double restitution for what he had defrauded—he was willing to repay four times what he had obtained by fraud!

Jesus' acts of table fellowship went beyond simply having a meal with Zacchaeus. He offered Zacchaeus grace in at least three ways. First, he tacitly pronounced forgiveness of Zacchaeus's sins. Second, he confirmed Zacchaeus as a "son of Abraham," that is as a member of the community in good standing. This was crucial. There was more at stake than personal forgiveness and relationship with Jesus. There was restoration to the community of faith. Third, Jesus challenged the faith community of his day to be as accepting as he was himself by receiving Zacchaeus as a community member, even though they had excluded him.

Jesus said that salvation had come to Zacchaeus's house. What did that salvation "do" for Zacchaeus?

Jesus' acts suggest another important understanding about discipleship. Prejudice is one of the great barriers to hospitality and results in exclusion. After all, we know "those people." That is, we know what kind of people they are (not "good folks" like us); and more, we know they aren't going to change. We exclude the possibility that they will ever be a part of the faith community.

The Dilemma of Table Fellowship in the Church: Galatians 2:11-14

The Dilemma of Table Fellowship in the Church ■

Read Galatians 2:11-14. Review the background material about the "council" in Jerusalem by reading Acts 15.

In the early church, table fellowship became an issue as disciples tried to be faithful to their understanding of what Jesus wanted them to do. This brief passage from Galatians gives us a glimpse of the stresses on the community in Antioch over hospitality. This was a major issue, in a major city. It involved some of the real "heavyweights" in the early church—Paul, Peter, and Barnabas. The basic question was, could one become a Christian without being a Jew first? Paul and Barnabas definitely said, "Yes." Others in Jerusalem said, "Absolutely not." The council, following the leadership of Peter and James, said, "Yes, but there are some minor requirements." Part of the requirements had to do with table fellowship.

Work out the narrative plot in Galatians 2:11-14. Who did what when? Who said what? What happened then?

Antioch was the third largest city in the Roman Empire. It was located in the province of Syria and was the military headquarters for the eastern frontier of the Empire. In addition, it was the shipping point for all the trade from the east—Armenia, Persia, and beyond. The Jewish historian Flavius Josephus says that Jews and Gentiles mixed freely together in the city, both economically and socially. So it was natural that Antioch would also become the base for the Christian mission to the Gentiles. If Jews and Gentiles could mix in society, why not in the church?

Earlier, a "council" in Jerusalem (see Acts 15) developed the terms for accepting Gentiles into what was still a predominantly Jewish-Christian church. In a multicultural community, challenges arose that the council could not anticipate. Further, there were different interpretations of what the council actually meant.

Paul understood that the agreement affirmed equality and table fellowship among Jews and Gentiles. Some of the stricter Jewish Christians saw it differently; they understood the agreement established an equal-but-separate Gentile mission, one in which the question of table fellowship would never arise. Given these differences, it was almost inevitable that there would be conflict. Antioch was the flash point.

It seems clear that, in the Antioch church, Jews and Gentiles ate together, at the same table. This is important to remember because the Lord's Supper was still being celebrated in the context of a community meal. Eating together meant that they also worshiped together. Why was this such a problem for Jewish Christians? After all, the Torah does not forbid Jews and Gentiles eating together. If everyone observed the minimal dietary precautions (see Acts 15), there was no obvious reason why even the strict literalists among the Jewish Christians could not eat with Gentile Christians. So what was the problem?

It is unlikely the conflict was over pork consumption. It seems clear that the first Gentile converts came from those who were already associated with the synagogues and worshiped the God of Israel (the so-called "God fearers"). They would already have been observing the basic dietary laws. It is more likely that the "men from James" objected to table fellowship itself. That is, they would not have been happy if the food had been triple-kosher—the idea of eating with Gentiles itself was offensive to them. Since this was the period of increased political tension leading up to the Jewish revolt against Rome, it may also have been that they wanted to be sure

Fill in the blank for people in your congregation: "The idea of eating with _____ is offensive to them." What words of direction would Paul (or Jesus) have for them?

there were no reasons to accuse the Christian movement of being anything less than fully loyal to Jewish tradition and to the Temple.

Principles or Personalities?

Principles or Personalities? ■

Based on what you know from reading the study book, Galatians 2:11-14, and Acts 15, develop an argument Peter might have made against Paul. Next, present Paul's side of the argument. After hearing both sides of the conflict, what compromise, if any, would you propose?

To what degree does the conflict seem related more to personality than principle? With whom would you have sided? Paul or Barnabas?

Whatever the reason, when the "men from James" raised the issue at Antioch, Peter waffled and Paul blew up. Peter's separation from table fellowship with Gentiles was a bow to the Jewish belief that the people of God should keep themselves free from contact with the Gentile world. This view of discipleship was marked by exclusion and separateness. Peter had already struggled with this in the vision recorded in Acts 10.

On the other hand, Peter had also been the pioneer in opening the church to the Gentiles (his meeting with Cornelius in Acts 10) and thus faced a dilemma. Peter was also the leader of the Jewish Christians in Antioch; so when he withdrew from table fellowship, many congregants went with him—including Barnabas, who was what we would call the "senior" pastor in the church. Paul and the Gentile Christians were excluded from their fellowship. The church was now split.

Paul argued that Peter and the others were caving in to pressure from the outside, instead of living up to their own basic convictions. Certainly in the case of Peter and Barnabas there seems to be some basis for his feeling. And we can imagine how deeply Paul must have been hurt by Barnabas's defection. Barnabas was the friend and companion who had brought him to Antioch to help in the leadership of the church and had joined him in preaching to the Gentiles. Personal feelings ran high, along with theological differences.

Paul gave Peter absolutely no credit for good motives. He did not even try to find out why

Peter did what he did. There was no attempt to resolve the conflict privately (see Matthew 18:15-17); rather, Paul saw Peter's actions as a denial of the gospel. To his mind, nothing was so important that it should divide the unity of the church. Of course, his own attitude could also be considered to be divisive.

To Paul, the bedrock issue was that Jewish Christians and Gentile Christians have fellowship with one another on equal terms. Of course, Paul's response also lacked acceptance—he attacked Peter personally. He charged Peter with caving in to pressure from the Jerusalem delegation, *and* that Peter was therefore requiring Gentile Christians to adhere to a higher standard of Torah observance than he himself would normally follow. When Peter, Barnabas, and the other Jewish Christians boycotted the common table, they were essentially forcing the Gentile Christians to adopt Jewish observances if they were to be included in the community. To Paul, this was a betrayal of the gospel.

It's easy, from a distance of nearly two thousand years, to be critical of both Peter and Paul in this situation. And yet, we have all seen, and participated in, divisions in the church where the only possible resolution for either party was for one side to win and the other side to lose. It is always possible to rationalize our actions on the highest grounds of faithfulness to the Scripture and to tradition. I've done that, as well; but I can't escape the feeling that, for Jesus, acceptance means tearing down walls rather than erecting barriers.

In spite of the common practice of the early church, there is nothing in Paul's language that suggests the Lord's Supper was involved. The issue was simply whether Jewish Christians and Gentile Christians could eat together under *any* circumstances,

"When we exclude others, we find that we are no longer relevant to them." What does that statement mean to you? If, for example, we exclude from the church persons below the official poverty line, how can the church be relevant to them? Or, if we exclude persons who are physically challenged (often because of the way our buildings are built), how are we relevant to them? If we exclude persons whose behavior seems sinful and immoral, how do we serve Christ in our relationship with others?

although this ultimately would have involved the Lord's Supper, since it was eaten in the context of a communal meal. For the first time, but certainly not for the last, the question of how one celebrates the Lord's Supper and who is invited, became a divisive issue in the church.

The story of Paul and Peter at Antioch reminds us of a hard lesson the church has had to learn over and over again, down through the centuries. When we exclude others, we find that we are no longer relevant to them. Why should anyone we have excluded choose to pay attention to us? The Holy Spirit moves where it will, continually calling us to be open and inclusive, rather than closed and exclusive. We make the greatest impact on the world when we stay at the table and listen to those with whom we disagree.

When we continue in conversation with those with whom we disagree, there is always the chance we will be able to bridge the differences. When we exclude those with whom we disagree, any chance for reconciliation is gone. When we disagree among ourselves, we serve the cause of Christ better when we continue to try to understand one another, rather than to shut others out. When we are at odds with secular society, we gain more by continuing to be in conversation with persons and institutions with whom we disagree. Simply "writing them off," as Paul seemed to do with Peter, will never win them to our cause.

Close With Prayer

This session has raised some issues that could be incendiary. In what ways could you invite members of the group to practice hospitality with one another in a situation of disagreement or anger?

O God of our church, we believe you did come for us, because we know we all sin and fall short in one way or another. Grant that our sin and weakness will not lead us to exclude others. Help us to practice the kind of acceptance that Jesus practiced—with ourselves, with one another, and with those outside our group, for whatever reason; in His name. Amen.

Session Three

Fasting

Session Focus ■

This session focuses on a subject modern Christians seldom discuss: fasting. New Testament and Christian tradition see fasting as an important spiritual discipline.

Session Objective ■

You will discover fasting as a spiritual discipline, how one fasts, the relationship of fasting to discipleship, and what the practice could mean for us today.

Session Preparation ■

Search through magazines, looking for advertisements that promise you painless ways to "get thin." Cut these out and make them into a collage to post in the room.

Choose from among these activities and discussion starters to plan your lesson.

Fasting ■

Point out the collage of weight-loss advertisements. Ask: What do they want us to do?

That seems strange! Isn't this a book about table fellowship? About throwing parties and welcoming people in? If it is, then why have a chapter on fasting? That seems out of place somehow. And, given the problems people have with bulimia and anorexia, why write about fasting?

Good questions. The reality is that, both in Jesus' day and in our own, people fast for the wrong reasons. Jesus offers some guidelines about fasting (or not fasting) that we need to look at carefully in the context of hospitality.

Most of us think of fasting in terms of weight loss. We want to "look good" for our class reunion, so we "fast" for a couple of weeks, hoping to drop a couple of waist sizes. Or, we think of fasting in terms of giving up chocolate, or something else we really like, for Lent—only to gorge on it Easter Day.

In the Judeo-Christian tradition, fasting has always been a spiritual discipline, a temporary physical sacrifice for the sake of our relationship with God. So fasting is not an end in itself; rather, it is a means that leads to a greater end. For some persons today, fasting is a way of both expressing solidarity with the poor and hungry, and providing food help for others. We fast (skip a meal or two) and contribute the money we would have spent on food to the local food bank, for example. Or, following the example of

Ask about fasting—or abstinence. In what contexts do we fast or abstain from certain things? during Lent? on doctor's orders? What have you learned about fasting as a spiritual discipline?

The Setting of the Story ■

Read this story in three Gospels (Matthew 9:14-17; Mark 2:18-22; Luke 5:33-39), and compare the three accounts. Are there significant differences? What were the practices of pious Jews in Jesus' day?

our United Methodist bishops, we abstain from food until three in the afternoon on Fridays, as an expression of solidarity with the poor. Time normally spent eating is spent in intercessory prayer.

In this chapter, we will look in some detail at one story about Jesus and fasting. This is the primary reference to fasting in the Gospels. The story is found in Matthew 9:14-17; Mark 2:18-22, and Luke 5:33-39. We will follow the outline of the story from Mark's Gospel, with references to Matthew and Luke.

The Setting of the Story

The actions of Jesus' disciples, on the one hand, and the disciples of John the Baptist and the Pharisees, on the other, are contrasted in this story. Fasting was an issue on which individual Jewish teachers often disagreed. Jewish tradition prescribed only one public fast each year: on the Day of Atonement or Yom Kippur (Leviticus 16:29-34).

The historical record, however, shows there had been times of public fasts in national emergencies. These fasts were usually proclaimed by the king, similar to a call by our presidents for a national day of prayer. Personal fasting by Jews was much more common. It was practiced as an expression of mourning, repentance, or supplication.

The normal practice of fasting meant more than simple abstention from food. The person fasting often wore sackcloth (a sign of mourning or repentance), ashes on the head, and did not bathe. This made a personal act of devotion a fairly public event. By the time of Jesus, fasting, prayer, and almsgiving were considered to be the signs of a righteous person. The Pharisees fasted twice a week, for example. Fasting was expected of any devout Jew.

Two additional points need to be made. First, Mark draws a clear distinction between the disciples of Jesus and those of John the Baptist. We know that, for several decades after John's death, his disciples continued as a separate Jewish sect. Mark (also Matthew and Luke) wanted to draw a sharp line between the two groups.

Second, the way Mark developed this story suggests that Christians do, indeed, fast; but they do not consider themselves bound by Jewish regulations or customs about fasting. By the end of the first century, for example, at least some Christians fasted two days a week, but deliberately chose days different from the fast days of the Pharisees.

The *Didache*, some parts of which were written as early as the split between the church and the synagogue (around A.D. 70), says, "But do not let your fasts coincide with those of the hypocrites. They fast on Monday and Thursday, so you must fast on Wednesday and Friday" (*Didache*, 8.1, in Michael Holmes, *The Apostolic Fathers*, page 259). The "hypocrites," of course, are the Pharisees; and the church is urged to fast on days different from the Pharisees, so they won't accidentally be mistaken for Pharisees.

The Pronouncement ■

What was there about weddings that made fasting inappropriate, even insulting? What's the relationship between a story about a wedding banquet and the situation in Jesus' life?

The Pronouncement: Mark 2:18-19a

Jesus responded to the question about fasting with a story. A common rhetorical device is to demonstrate the absurdity of the opponent's argument. This device was commonly used by Jewish rabbis to interpret Torah. Jesus responded fully within the rabbinic tradition of his time (at least as far as we know it). Wedding guests don't fast during the wedding they celebrate. In the rabbinic tradition, a wedding feast takes precedence over almost every other religious obligation. Bridegrooms were excused from military duty until after the honeymoon; rabbis were excused from the study of Torah for the wedding feast. Certainly fasting could be put aside.

Social etiquette is also involved here, which puts fasting in a negative light. Fasting, as we have seen, was a public gesture of mourning or repentance. For guests to fast (wear sackcloth and ashes, not bathe, not eat) at a wedding would make it seem they were disapproving of the wedding. This would be a serious insult to the host.

So? Jesus' presence is like a wedding banquet. It is a time of great celebration, the anticipation of the great wedding banquet of the Messiah. Just as wedding guests don't fast at the banquet, Jesus' disciples don't fast in the presence of the Messiah. The new age of the kingdom of God is present in Jesus, and fasting is not appropriate—one does not insult the Messiah at the Messiah's own banquet! In this narrative, Mark provides an explanation for why Christians observed fasting even though it is clear that Jesus and his disciples did not fast.

The *Gospel of Thomas* (Logion 104) has an interesting variation on this story. When Jesus is asked why he does not fast, he replies that fasting would suggest he is a sinner. Then Jesus says the disciples may fast when the bridegroom leaves. There are two different things being said here. The reference to fasting when the bridegroom leaves carries the same meaning as the Synoptic (Matthew, Mark, and Luke) sayings. There is also a different understanding of who Jesus is. Notice the contrast between Mark's understanding

Who makes any public display of fasting in our time? How might public fasting (e.g., Gandhi's hunger strikes) make a necessary statement in our world?

of Jesus as the one who begins the new age and the Thomas emphasis on the sinlessness of Jesus. The Thomas interpretation (the sinlessness of Jesus) represents an entirely different understanding. But the two sayings have the one important element in common—the disciples cannot fast while Jesus is with them.

The Time to Fast ■

When is fasting appropriate for us? In what different ways can we fast?

What are some ways in which abstinence could be an important spiritual discipline for us?

The Time to Fast: Mark 2:19b-20

Since Mark (also Matthew and Luke) thinks of Jesus as the bridegroom in the story, these verses remind us that, in fact, Jesus will be taken away. The time of celebration is lived in the shadow of the passion and death of the Messiah. After his death, his disciples will have plenty of time to fast. The "on that day" of verse 20 probably indicates a time when fasting is appropriate and not the specific day on which Jesus was taken from them.

When Mark was written, Christians were living in the time when fasting was appropriate. The bridegroom had been taken away. Even with the reality of the Resurrection, the literal physical presence of Christ was gone from their midst. He was in glory with the Father, until the return. So fasting was an appropriate spiritual discipline. It was not necessarily a sign of mourning, but a longing for the coming of the Lord.

Fasting may be a sign of repentance, or a special preparation for prayer. Abstinence is also a spiritual discipline. In some Christian traditions, abstinence has meant not eating meat or pleasant food on certain days or during Lent.

John Wesley, the founder of Methodism, urged his followers to practice fasting or abstinence for the sake of spiritual discipline. This allowed them more time for prayer and

Bible 301 ☐

Covenant together to fast one meal a week for a set period of time (two weeks, one month, during Lent). Search for prayers and Scriptures to read while you fast. Meet during this period to support one another. Meet again after the fasting period to tell of your experiences.

more money to give to the poor. Wesley included abstinence from liquor or certain foods as a substitute for fasting. He considered both to be appropriate spiritual disciplines.

Jesus' Rules for Fasting ■

Jesus' Rules for Fasting: Matthew 6:16-18

What is the definition of *fasting*? Does that fit with your understanding?

A fast is a "voluntary abstention from food for a prescribed period as a sign of devotion" (*New Interpreter's Bible*, Vol. VIII, page 205). Jesus was not opposed to fasting as a spiritual discipline, only to its inappropriate use. We know that Jesus himself fasted. The Synoptic Gospels (Matthew, Mark, and Luke) all tell us that, after his baptism, Jesus fasted and prayed for forty days in the wilderness, seeking to comprehend his calling from God. Clearly, he did not completely abstain from food and water for forty full days. Probably, like many monks in the early Christian tradition, he ate only one meal a day, perhaps a small piece of bread or some wild fruit, and drank water. So, for clear and compelling reasons, Jesus would endorse fasting.

Read the story of the Temptation (in Matthew 4:1-11). What do you think fasting meant for Jesus? What was he seeking by his fast?

As a part of the teachings collected in what we call the "Sermon on the Mount," Jesus laid down some guidelines for his disciples to use in fasting. What he suggested was exactly the opposite of the way fasting was practiced by many fellow Jews. Jesus' point was to decide whether one fasts as acts of devotion to impress others or as acts of devotion to God. The disciples were told to act normally when they fasted, so that only God would be aware of their devotion.

Remind yourself again what were the practices of fasting in Jesus' day. In contrast, how did he want his own disciples to fast?

If we were to fast, what would we seek to gain from it?

Jesus' warning against ostentatious fasting must not become an excuse to abandon this devotion and spiritual discipline. Jesus never said we should not practice our piety—he just told us to not do it to impress fellow humans!

On our second trip to Israel, I was reminded of what Jesus meant. We were on a jumbo jet, together with a large number of Orthodox Jews. It was an overnight flight and, early in the morning, the Orthodox men began binding the prayer boxes on their foreheads and arms, shaking out their prayer shawls, and praying aloud. My first (private, midwestern, Protestant) reaction was that this was pretty ostentatious and exactly the kind of thing that Jesus told his disciples not to do. Then it dawned on me that they were praying and I wasn't! Further, they didn't care whether I watched them or not, whether I was impressed or not. What mattered to them was that they had a spiritual obligation to fulfill, and they intended to do it. I was rebuked and chastened by my own reflection on my own attitude and did, in fact, pause and pray quietly.

Proverbs About the Old and New ■

How do these sayings (in Mark 2:21-22, for example) "raise the bar" on the question of spiritual discipline? How do they apply to our spiritual disciplines and the way in which we relate to God in Jesus Christ?

Proverbs About the Old and New: Mark 2:21-22

These sayings about the old and the new move from a specific confrontation about fasting to a more generalized statement about spiritual practices. They also "raise the bar" on the question of spiritual discipline. The illustration seems perfectly clear—if you sew a piece of new, unshrunk, cloth on an old shirt, when the new piece shrinks it will rip out stitches, tear the cloth, and make the hole even worse. Luke has an interesting variation on the saying. He talks about cutting a patch from a new garment and sewing it on the old one. Luke presents two problems. The first problem is the same as in Mark and Matthew. When the patch from the new garment shrinks, it will make the hole worse. The second problem in Luke's version states that not only is the hole in the old garment made worse, one has also ruined the new garment, with no benefit to the old one.

What does all that mean? For Luke, the challenge is to see Jesus and his teachings as a new garment. One should not cut up the new garment to patch the old one. It would be better to throw away the old one, rather than ruin them both. By implication, Luke defines fasting as the "old garment." Luke seems to dismiss the necessity of fasting.

The same thinking applies to the wineskins. An old wineskin is likely to be brittle, and not able to expand when new wine ferments. The fermentation process breaks the old wineskin, spills (and ruins) the wine, and leaves nothing. It is better to put new wine into new wineskins. By analogy, Jesus and his teachings are new wine. One should not try to fit them into the old wineskins of fixed religious practices.

The Synoptic Gospels were written (in their present form) after A.D. 75, when the Jewish revolt against Rome was finally put down. Prior to this time, Christians had been identified by the Romans as a Jewish sect. But the Christians, who had no part in the revolt, no longer wanted to be identified with a people and a faith that was defined as hostile to Rome. This led to the final split between church and synagogue. It may be that the teachings about new wine and new garments reflect something of the break between Jewish tradition and Christian faith. Christian communities concluded it was better to stay with the new wine and give up most of the traditions and practices of their Jewish heritage.

What are some solid spiritual reasons for fasting? If we choose to fast, are there some ways we could do it in community, so that we could support one another in faithfulness?

Close With Prayer ■

Gracious God, Jesus reminded us to practice our piety by offering it to you rather than displaying it in such a way that others notice us. Help us to live our piety in such a way that people see us and our goodness rather than our piety; through Jesus Christ, who came to make his heavenly Father known to us. Amen.

And What About Us?

Many contemporary Christian leaders are reluctant to recommend fasting as a spiritual discipline. This comes out of an awareness of our society's obsession with being thin and the fear of serious health problems stemming from anorexia and bulimia. Neither of those, of course, represents fasting in the traditional sense; but they are warnings about fasting inappropriately. How would one fast today?

First, the Gospels are clear. One fasts for spiritual reasons. One can fast as a sign of commitment to spiritual discipline. This kind of fast can lead to extra time spent in prayer for the problems caused by hunger in the world; it can lead to a keener awareness of God in our lives; it can lead us to take specific action to deal with hunger. The key is that we fast as a sign of devotion.

Second, one fasts carefully. A friend once told me that he tried fasting as a spiritual discipline, but discovered that by late afternoon, his brain was doing "funny things" to him. It is better to approach fasting carefully, perhaps giving up lunch, or eating smaller amounts of food. In addition, fasting does not mean we dehydrate ourselves. Water, perhaps fruit juice, should always be drunk, even in periods of fasting. One does not serve God by endangering one's health.

Session Four

Miracle Meals

Session Focus ■

This session will focus on two "miracle meals," those times when fasting was possible only because of events far out of the ordinary.

Session Objective ■

You will see how two of Jesus' miracles open the door to the discipleship as well as table fellowship. They also point beyond themselves to the messianic feast and the Eucharist.

Session Preparation ■

Several activities suggest looking at Old Testament roots of the New Testament stories. Read those stories carefully before the session. If you choose to use the video, *Jesus of Nazareth*, be sure you have the videocassette cued and a VCR in place. For the closing activity you will need to research newspapers, news magazines, or the Internet for information on overwhelming crises in today's world.

Choose from among these activities and discussion starters to plan your lesson.

The Wedding Feast at Cana: John 2:1-12

We recently had another wedding in our extended family, when our nephew married a wonderful young woman. The reception was quite a party! There was feasting and music and family and friends sharing their lives with each other. Indeed, for some, the party lasted well into the night. But even that party was nothing like wedding receptions in Jesus' day. The usual festivities included a procession in which the groom's friends brought the bride to the groom's house and a wedding buffet. The celebration lasted seven days! Some scholars suggest that, since the feasting went on so long, guests were expected to bring their share of the food and drink, just as we all bring food to the church potluck. This would be a sign of hospitality, in that all share to make the feast a success.

These scholars suggest that Jesus and his disciples came for the feast, but brought nothing with them. This caused a shortage in crucial supplies, including the wine—which sets the stage for the first "sign" or miracle in John's Gospel. This first sign is (for John's Gospel) the beginning of Jesus' ministry—and a physical sign of the gift he has to offer humanity.

The "three days" probably mean three days after the day referred to in John 1:43. We'd like to know for sure, and to know

Ask persons in the group to share stories about the last wedding or family feast they attended. What happened around the table, as people ate and drank together?

Read together John 2:1-12. Point out the word *sign* in the story. We'll come back to "signs" later, but point out that there was more to the story than just changing water into wine. The sign pointed to a deeper and more profound reality.

about several other details as well, but the Gospel writer was not interested in the kind of detail questions we like to raise. He subordinates all those details to the sign itself. So let's turn to the sign.

Mary, Jesus' mother, came to Jesus with the problem. This may indicate that she was aware Jesus and his friends were a part of the problem and wanted him to resolve it. Jesus' answer seems incredibly distant: "What concern is that to you and me? My hour has not yet come" (2:4).

Hour is a technical term in John's Gospel, referring to Jesus' passion, death, resurrection, and ascension. Jesus' response moves this conversation beyond the immediate story to a broader theological context. Later, the Gospel writer will make it clear that Jesus was free from human control, even in the hour of his death.

Mary seemed certain that Jesus would do something, even though he resists her urging. She told the household servants to do whatever Jesus said, which raises, for us, the interesting and unanswerable question of how Mary had authority over the servants in someone else's home. Was this a family wedding, in which aunts sometimes have a great deal of authority?

That's a Lot of Wine!

Water was stored in stone jars for use in purification rites. Stone jars were used because if they became ritually contaminated, they could be cleaned. Pottery jars could not and would have to be broken (see Leviticus 11:29-38). The size of the jars puts the spotlight on the extravagance of the sign. Each of these jars had a capacity of 20 to 30 gallons, so Jesus provided some 120 to 180 gallons of wine! That is, truly, a *lot* of wine!

At the heart of the sign is a wild, divine, extravagance.

What does it all mean? Some have argued that the water for ritual purification represents the old order of Jewish tradition and the wine the new order of Christ. But there is no indication here of a rejection of Jewish tradition. This is not like "new wine in new wineskins," where the point is clearly replacing the old with the new; rather, we would be better served to see the wine as the creation of something new *in the midst of Jewish life*.

The Christian community gathered around the writer of this Gospel wanted to continue to remain within the Jewish community, and they fought against separation. In the end, the Johannine community was driven out of the synagogue. They did not depart willingly. So this Gospel is not going to give any indications that Jesus repudiated his religious heritage. There is something new here, but not something that rejects or replaces Jewish faith.

Saving the Best Till Last ■

This was apparently a kind of "hospitality maxim," one that describes how canny hosts cut expenses. Invite group members to read Amos 9:13 and Joel 3:18 to get a sense of the scriptural significance of an abundance of *good* wine.

Saving the Best Till Last

Saving the best till last—how often have we heard some variation of that saying? It is a saying that runs counter to conventional practice, apparently. The steward's first words after he tasted the water turned into wine may be a sort of "hospitality maxim." You serve the good wine first and save the poor stuff until last, when the guests have indulged enough they no longer can tell the difference. That would make a certain amount of sense, if funds were limited. The steward didn't know where this wine came from and assumed that the bridegroom was following this old maxim. So it is no wonder that he was surprised when he tasted the wine—the bridegroom had gone against all social custom by saving the good wine until last. Then there was that interesting little aside—the servants did know where the wine came from. They were impartial witnesses to the sign.

The steward's surprise works as a part of the story. The surprise also works as a witness to the deeper truth. God saved the best until the coming of Christ. Jesus Christ is the best God has to offer the world.

In the Hebrew Scripture, an abundance of wine is a symbol of the last days, when God would bring a new richness to the world. Amos 9:13, for example, says that the very mountains will drip wine and the hills flow with it. Joel 3:18 also refers to mountains dripping sweet wine and hills flowing with milk (another sign of God's coming). So, on one level, the author of John is saying that Jesus brings to completion and fulfillment all the hopes of the Hebrew Scripture for God's richness. "The best" has come at the last.

Because John's Gospel is so interested in the Eucharist, it is natural that we would look for references to Eucharist in this story. The original hearers of the Gospel would hear about the abundance of wine and immediately think about the abundance of wine in God's coming kingdom. This would, in turn, remind them of the wine of the Eucharist, which is a meal about the Kingdom.

Signs and Their Purpose

In our world, signs give directions. Either they tell us to do something (Stop, Yield, Slow Down) or they point us in the right direction (parking, hospital, restrooms, restaurants). In either case, they point to a reality beyond themselves. That's what signs do in John's Gospel. The sign itself is impor-

Signs and Their Purpose ■

What is the usual function for a sign? What was the most unusual sign you ever saw? Did you ever miss an important turn because a sign was missing? What do signs do in John's Gospel? Can you see ways in which these signs could reveal to you Jesus' glory and lead you to believe in him?

tant, but what it points to is much more important.

That's the point we often miss in the modern world. We expend a great deal of energy trying to explain "how" Jesus was able to perform the signs. The truth is, knowing how a sign was provided would not increase our understanding of the meaning of the sign. The signs shattered all conventional wisdom, reason, and expectation. It is that "shattering" on which we need to focus. Jesus did something that defies conventional reason and normal expectations.

Signs have a dual function in this Gospel (see verse 11). They reveal Jesus' glory, and they lead his disciples to believe in him. What is most important is not the signs themselves, but the revelation they bring and the response they awaken. "Revealed his glory" means that Jesus revealed he was the *Logos*, the divine Son, who has come to earth as a human being. This is the expression in the life of the disciples of the glory described in the great hymn of John 1:1-18.

Believing does not mean giving intellectual assent, as in "Yes, I believe that's true." It is "betting our lives" that it is true and living differently as a result.

The Feeding of the Five Thousand: Mark 6:30-44; 8:1-9; Matthew 14:13-21; 15:32-39; Luke 9:10-17; John 6:1-13

The Feeding of the Five Thousand

This is the only wonder story found in all four Gospels. Read the accounts (Mark 6:30-44, 8:1-9; Matthew 14:13-21; 15:32-39; Luke 9:10-17; and John 6:1-13) and compare the details.

This is the only sign that is found in all four Gospels. In fact, it is found six times, since the story of the feeding of the four thousand in Mark and Matthew is probably a doublet of the feeding of the five thousand. There are many references to Hebrew Scripture in the story. Mark tells us that Jesus had compassion on the crowd, because they were like sheep without a shepherd. In

If you are studying this book in a group, form teams, one to read each story. Make a list of parallels on a chalkboard or piece of poster paper.

Show the segment of the video "Jesus of Nazareth" that portrays the feeding of the five thousand. Compare the video to what you read in the Gospels. How significant are the differences?

Bible 301 □

The early disciples celebrated the Lord's Supper by eating a complete meal as a congregation. At the beginning of the meal, the bishop took bread, blessed, broke, and gave it to all. After the meal, the bishop took the cup, blessed it, and all drank from the cup to complete the meal. This ancient practice could be incorporated in a church potluck.

Ask the pastor to begin the meal by taking, blessing, breaking, and giving the bread to all at the meal. When all have shared in the breaking of the bread, the pastor can offer ex tempore prayers to consecrate each item of food.

When the meal is over, the pastor blesses the cup, and all can conclude by sharing in the cup and saying a

Hebrew Scripture, God is described as the good shepherd. Kings are called to be shepherds (to act as God would act) for their people. Moses prayed for a shepherd for the Israelites (Numbers 27:17); the prophets condemned kings for failing to act as shepherds (1 Kings 22:17); Ezekiel 34 is a long discourse on the failure of Israel's leaders to shepherd the people and God as the true shepherd. Jesus was a shepherd by healing and teaching the crowds. Shepherds also feed their sheep, so the feeding of the five thousand fits well into the theme of table fellowship.

John tells us that "the Passover was at hand." In John's Gospel, this story serves the same purpose as the Last Supper in the Synoptic Gospels—it is the institution of the Eucharist. So it would be important for John to tell the story in a Passover setting.

The disciples, in all three Synoptic accounts (Matthew, Mark, and Luke), ask Jesus to send the crowds away so they can find food and lodging. The dialogue is familiar—Jesus told them to take care of the problem, and they were incredulous. How in the world could they do this?

This part of the story, too, has a parallel with the Hebrew Scripture. The Israelites in the wilderness grumbled because they were hungry and doubted that God could feed them; here the disciples were doubtful. Mark and John report that the disciples estimated it would take 200 *denarii* to buy bread for the crowd, and even then there would be only a small taste for each person. A *denarius* was the standard day's wage for a working person, so they were aware that feeding the multitude would require seven months' wages. Instead, Jesus asked them what resources were available. In John's Gospel, prayer of thanksgiving. In the early church, the deacons collected all the food remaining at the end of the meal and took it to the widows and orphans. In this way, the action of worship to God and service to others was combined in a single sacrament. The potluck meal with Eucharist could include acts to relieve the needs of the poor.

How do those passages enrich your understanding of Mark's comment that Jesus had compassion on the crowds because they were like sheep without a shepherd?

Look at Some Old Testament Roots ■

There are Old Testament roots that would have been in the minds of the first readers of the Gospels as they heard or read these stories. Take some time to look at those roots and see how they enrich your

Jesus initiated the conversation by asking Philip how they would buy bread for all the people; but the end result was the same.

One of the traditional ways interpreters have tried to deal with this miraculous event is to suggest that, when the multitude discovered only five loaves and two fish were available, everyone was so embarrassed that they finally brought out the food they had hidden away and then shared it with others. This is *not* what the Gospel writers say, and it is *not* the point of the story. Sharing is an important virtue, one we supposedly learn in kindergarten; but this is a story about God's gracious provision, not about sharing.

The meal was extraordinary—look at the statistical details! Mark, John, and Luke say there were "five thousand men" in the crowd. Matthew says "five thousand men, besides women and children." In other words, a huge crowd. Jesus commanded them to sit down on the grass. This was placing the multitude at table with him as their host. It is the same way the banquet host invites his guests to be seated. These people were about to be Jesus' guests at a wonderful meal. Look at more statistics. They all ate enough to be satisfied, and there were twelve baskets full of leftovers. We can assume these were fairly large baskets, not little ones the size of offering plates; so there were lots of leftovers.

Look at Some Old Testament Roots

Let's look beyond the story to some of the references and connotations first-century readers would pick up on almost automatically. First, the miracle was given around Passover time—John is probably correct in this. Its place in the religious calendar would have brought to mind the divine provision of understanding of the story.

Shepherd Images:
Psalm 23;
Numbers 27:17;
1 Kings 22:17;
Ezekiel 34.

The Israelites grumbled in the wilderness because they didn't have food (Exodus 16:1-21). The prophet Elisha fed a crowd with only a few loaves (2 Kings 4:42-44.)

Note the fourfold action of Jesus. What does it have to do with the Eucharist?

The Eucharist Today ■

Why did the disciples doubt that Jesus could feed the crowd? What did Jesus want the disciples to do? Are there times in our lives when we know that we should make an extra effort and do good for someone else, but we're just tired and want to get home and rest?

Gather data on the AIDS crisis in Africa and India. Check out archived articles at *www.newyorktimes.com* or *www.pbs.org* on the Internet. Bring those and similar articles to the session. Distribute the articles, and ask individuals to scan them quickly. Ask for first impressions on the depth of the problem. Remind them that the disciples felt over-

manna for the Hebrew children as they wandered in the wilderness for forty years (Exodus 16). Passover itself was a miracle of liberation, and God's people continued to celebrate it as God's mighty act. The manna was a miracle, and the memory of it remained strong in the faith of Israel.

Second, the feeding of the multitude recalled the prophet Elisha feeding one hundred men with twenty loaves (2 Kings 4:42-44). Finally, the fourfold formula about Jesus taking, blessing, breaking, and giving the bread recalled the action that occurred in the institution of the Eucharist. In the early church, the Eucharist was celebrated primarily in the context of a common meal; every act of table fellowship was thus a reminder of the Eucharist.

The Eucharist Today

In the church today, we use language about being invited to the Lord's Table. Many of us still vividly remember the words printed on an old poster: "Jesus of Nazareth invites you to a banquet held in his honor," with a background depicting a loaf of bread and a cup. The early church ate together and celebrated the Eucharist together as an anticipation of the great banquet of the Messiah in God's kingdom.

What kind of difference would it make in our churches if, every time we celebrated Holy Communion, we saw it as a foretaste of the Kingdom? Would we be more or less willing to receive regularly? Would we be more or less open to "them" joining us at the table? Or what about church potlucks? What difference might it make in the life of the church if we consciously and deliberately talked about all those covered dishes, and the time we spent talking as we ate them, as a sign of the whelmed when Jesus told them to provide food for the crowd. Ask: What do you think Jesus would say to us about this situation? What could we do to at least make a start on solving the problem?

Gather articles about hungry children in the United States, or about children (and adults) who have no health insurance. (See the same Internet sources as above, if you don't find articles in your local paper.) Follow the same process as outlined for the AIDS crisis above.

Close With Prayer ■

God of compassion, the needs of the world overwhelm us, and we feel like the disciples—what can we do about such a big problem? Give us guidance, we pray, and courage to take risks to help the helpless of our world. As we receive the bread of heaven when we commune at the Table of our Lord, may we receive power to feed the hungry souls and bodies that are all around us; through Christ the living bread that came from heaven. Amen.

Kingdom? Would we eat and drink differently? Would we see each other differently?

Looking at the deeper levels of the story, both Jesus' teaching and providing food demonstrate that he is the true shepherd for God's people. He met their need for physical food in the miraculous feeding. His words provided them their source of eternal life. The church continues to feed soul and body. Teaching, preaching, Sunday school, Bible studies, vacation Bible school, are essential parts of the ministry of the church.

Providing food is also an essential part of the ministry of the church. We are called to feed the hungry. We look at all the physical needs in today's world—for food, clean drinking water, medical care, clothing, and housing—and like the disciples ask: Do you know how much it would cost to provide even a basic minimum for all these needs? The bill for dealing with AIDS in sub-Saharan Africa and in India alone is projected to run into the billions of dollars. Can we hear Jesus saying to us: "You take care of it"?

John's Gospel ends the story by saying that the people saw the *sign* and said, "This is indeed the prophet who is to come into the world" (John 6:14). There was a common strand of expectation that God would raise up a "prophet-like-Moses" who would again save God's people. This sign of the feeding helped them recognize that Jesus was Messiah.

Session Five

The Bread of Life

Session Focus ◼

The primary focus of this session is on the bread metaphor. The secondary focus is on the Eucharist, or Lord's Supper.

Session Objective ◼

Persons involved in this session will come away with (1) a new understanding of how the writer of John's Gospel uses dialogue as a teaching tool; (2) a new appreciation of the bread metaphor in Jesus' teaching, and (3) a deepened appreciation for the Eucharist.

Session Preparation ◼

Read John 6 carefully, thinking about the questions that the crowd raises, and note how Jesus responds to the issues rather than to the questions of the crowd. Read the material in this chapter carefully, so you will have the issues firmly in your mind.

Many adult groups manage to have coffee as a part of their routine. Add a special surprise, fresh-baked bread and an ample supply of butter.

"I don't get anything out of it."

"What is supposed to happen?"

"I wish we didn't do it so often."

"I like the quiet time at the Communion rail."

"It's the most important thing we ever do in worship. I hate it when I have to miss."

"This morning I read the parts of the liturgy the pastor leaves out. They're beautiful. I wish he'd include them."

(Comments from an informal poll after worship, asking how people feel about Holy Communion.)

What does happen in Communion (the Lord's Supper, Eucharist)? And what should we expect to "get out of it"? These are common questions for Christians in our day. In this chapter, we will explore what happens in table fellowship and how that relates to what happens between us and Jesus Christ in Communion. First, table fellowship.

Last week, I received a note from my cousin, inviting my wife and me to lunch. Her sister-in-law and nieces were going to be there, and she wanted us to get together. The key line in her note was "some of the best things happen around the table." That's true for many of us. Some of the most important times of the entire year are when the family eats together—Thanksgiving, Christmas, family reunions. We actually take

You will need copies of your church's Communion liturgy for a Bible 301 activity.

Choose from among these activities and discussion starters to plan your lesson.

Eat and Drink ■

Provide coffee, tea, and sliced, fresh-baked bread and butter (or a low-fat spread). Eat and drink together, simply enjoying the taste of bread and coffee and the delight of one another's company.

When the group gathers, ask: What difference did it make to our sense of community that we stopped and ate and talked together? What does table fellowship make possible?

They Didn't Get It, Either ■

Look at the "discourse pattern" in John's Gospel, which is described in the first paragraph.

Invite your group to see how that pattern works out in John 6:25-59. Outline those verses in light of the "discourse pattern." How does each additional statement Jesus makes add to the theological understanding of bread, feeding the five thousand, and the Eucharist?

time to be present to each other, to share stories about life and hope and memories. The food is not nearly as important as the time we spend together.

The same thing is true when the church family eats together. We don't get to talk to everyone at the church picnic or potluck supper, but we do take time to be present to one another and share stories and hopes. It's an easy step from there to fellowship at the Lord's Table. We eat together, we share memories of the faith (in the Great Thanksgiving), and we take time to be present to God in Jesus Christ. Unfortunately, as the comments at the beginning of the chapter show, not everyone feels the same way about what's happening.

They Didn't Get It, Either

John's Gospel tells us that not everyone who was present at the feeding of the five thousand "got it." In fact, he says they followed Jesus back to Capernaum and asked him lots of questions. The familiar pattern in John's Gospel is that someone asks a question, which Jesus seems not to answer. They don't "get" his answer and ask another question, which leads to another discourse about the meaning of what is going on. Let's see how this pattern works in John 6:25-59.

The first question (verse 25) seems strange. "When did you come here?" has nothing to do with the sequence of events. And Jesus' response is not an answer to what they asked, although it may have been an answer to what they meant. Now that the crowd was confused, Jesus spoke words of eternal significance.

What is "food that endures for eternal life"? Obviously, it is different from the bread and fish with which Jesus fed the crowd. This is similar to the conversation with the Samaritan woman (John 4) about water that quenches thirst forever. Both food that endures for eternal life and water that quenches thirst forever are metaphors about eternal life. They remind the reader that Jesus' followers are called to seek for more lasting things than the next meal or drink. The question about priorities, particularly spiritual priorities, is crucial for Christians in all times and places.

Then Jesus says the Father has set his seal on the Son of Man. To "set a seal" on something is to give it a formal mark of identification. In ancient times, documents marked with a seal were accepted as authentic messages from the one who sealed them. In Christian practice, baptism has been seen as a "seal," by which we were marked through the work of the Holy Spirit. In this conversation, "setting a seal" means that God has marked the Son of Man as God's own. This increases the significance of the conversation. It's about more than just bread. It is about the salvation that the Son has come into the world to bring. At least, we can understand this when we read the story.

In contrast, the crowd didn't get it. They took the statement about life as a gift and asked what works they needed to be doing. Jesus tried to center the conversation back on grace by re-defining *work*. Jesus defined *work* not as something done, but as faith in Jesus himself. We expend a lot of energy trying to figure out what we can do to please God. Jesus said God wants us to have faith that Jesus is God's Son.

But What Have You Done for Me Lately?

It was Friday evening at the District Youth Institute. The youth leaders of the district were doing a "Saturday Night Live"-style

How does the information about a "seal" "raise the bar" on the conversation? If God set a "seal" on Jesus, how did Jesus understand that seal in terms of his mission? How does the seal God sets on us in our baptism lead us to discipleship, mission, and service to the world?

But What Have You Done for Me Lately?

Part of the "discourse pattern" is that Jesus and the crowd use the same words with different meanings. What does the crowd mean by *works*? What does Jesus mean?

What does the crowd mean by *signs*? What does Jesus mean? What different levels of meaning do you detect in this dialogue?

presentation on the cross and the meaning of the cross. One youth was standing in a pulpit, thundering (like an old-time evangelist), "Jesus died for your sins!" Another youth walked across in front of him, saying, "Yeah, but what has he done for me lately?" We sometimes get that feeling, don't we? All the talk about Jesus saving us relates to events of long ago, and we'd like to know what's happening now. That's where the crowd was in John's account of the dialogue. Sure, you fed us manna, but what have you done for us lately?

The crowd and Jesus used the same words, but with very different meanings. The crowd wanted Jesus to "do a work." They were willing to do God's work—but only if Jesus did God's work first and gave them a sign. They didn't recognize that Jesus had just given them a sign. The loaves and fishes were not enough: They asked for manna!

So Jesus patiently reminded them of some eternal truths behind the giving of the manna and the bread:

- It was God, not Moses, who gave the bread;
- The gift of bread happens now, not in the past;
- The bread of God is that which comes down from heaven;
- The ones who receive the true bread are those given to Jesus by the Father.

Look at the conversation again, as it is recorded in your Bible. On how many levels do you see the conversation operating?

Jesus' "I am" Statements

- *I am the bread of life (John 6:35)*
- *I am the light of the world (8:12)*
- *I am the door for the sheep (10:7, 9)*
- *I am the good shepherd (10:11, 14)*
- *I am the resurrection and the life (11:25)*
- *I am the way, the truth, and the life (14:6)*
- *I am the true vine (15:1, 5)*

The First Discourse ■

There are six other "I am" sayings in John's Gospel. Form teams, and ask each team to read one of the other sayings—and enough of the context to see how the metaphor works in their particular saying. Invite the teams to report on their metaphors and how they work. Record the reports on chalkboard or posterboard. Ask: What does each metaphor suggest about who Jesus is? about how he works in our lives? about discipleship?

What does it mean to say that "Jesus will never drive away those who believe in him"? What does that suggest to us about our own salvation?

The First Discourse: John 6:35-40

This is one of the great "I am" sayings in the Gospel. In Hebrew, the verb *I am* is the same root as the divine name (see Exodus 3:13). In each of these sayings, Jesus is identified with God—and as the fulfillment of the metaphor (bread, light, door, and so on). In John 6, the metaphor is bread, with a clear reference back to the water in John 4. Bread and water are the most fundamental needs for human life, and Jesus identified himself with them. So here we have some basic clues about what "he's done for us lately," what happens when we are given faith to confess Jesus as God's Son:

1. Our basic human needs and religious longings are met in him. Those who believe in him (still following the metaphor) will never be hungry or thirsty.

2. Jesus will never drive away those who believe in him. This is a powerful word of grace for a world and a people all too aware of alienation. When we no longer satisfy the demands of an employer, we are terminated. When we no longer please another person in a relationship, we are ignored. Jesus promises that all who are given to him by the Father will never be lost by him.

3. God's purpose for salvation is to bring

humanity to Jesus and to all the life that Jesus offers.

4. God's will for salvation is inclusive—"anyone who comes to me." This cannot be overemphasized. Over and over in these few verses, Jesus says that God's will is that no one should be lost, but raised up on the Day of Judgment. God's will is that *anyone* who sees the Son and believes in him will have eternal life. The *anyone* is crucial. For John's Gospel, seeing and believing are at the heart of faith. To see clearly is to believe.

I'm From Missouri—Show Me!

The crowd heard the discourse and responded in disbelief. They grumbled, just as their ancestors did in the wilderness. How in the world, they wanted to know, could Jesus be the true bread from heaven, when he came from Nazareth? They knew his parents; how could he claim to come from God? On one level, we are amazed they didn't understand what was going on. On another level, we're all from Missouri. We want to be shown. The things that are seen are things that can be known; the things that are not seen belong to faith.

The Second Discourse: John 6:43-52

Most of what Jesus says here repeats the themes of the first discourse. It is God who draws people to Jesus. God makes faith possible for all people. There is the need for a faith response to God's action—one must hear and learn from the Father and come to Jesus. Earlier, we became aware that seeing and believing are metaphors for how humans respond to God. Hearing and learning also are metaphors for that response. In the Hebrew Scripture "to hear" means something like "to take into oneself and act on

I'm From Missouri—Show Me! ■

The crowd is sure that Jesus can't be who he claims to be, because they know his parents. We all want to be shown, don't we? "There is a fine line . . . between critical thinking and discernment on the one hand, and outright skepticism and rejection on the other." How do we know where that "fine line" is? How can we know whether we are being discerning or skeptical?

The Second Discourse ■

This section of the discourse focuses our attention on the Eucharist, with the language about the "bread from heaven." Remind participants that, in the last session, you talked about the manna, which was a kind of bread from heaven. What does Jesus mean here when he uses that language?

Invite the group to read the hymn in the Prologue to the Gospel (John 1:1-18). Then write on the chalkboard or on posterboard, side by side, the words "bread from heaven" and "the Word became flesh." Ask: What is the connection, for faith, between these two phrases? Encourage group members to read John 6:43-52 again. How does the "I am" metaphor relate to "the Word became flesh"?

Then ask: What happens in the Eucharist? What does the text suggest? What is the reality you experience at the Lord's table? How does Christ draw close to us in the Eucharist? What draws us closer to each other? What is vitally important in this meal to both our personal spiritual lives and the life of the community?

what one has heard," or "to hear is to obey." And what is it that the crowd must hear and learn? Jesus is the bread of life; all who believe in him receive eternal life.

So far, we haven't dealt directly with the questions about the Eucharist with which we opened the chapter; but we've been talking about it all along. The whole conversation about bread is in the context of Eucharist. We saw, in John 4, that the feeding of the five thousand possesses eucharistic overtones. And now we hear about the "bread from heaven."

This "bread from heaven" reminds us first of the great hymn in the Prologue to the Gospel (John 1:1-18). There we read that the Word became flesh and dwelt among us (1:14). Here we read about the "flesh" in the context of the Eucharist. In the metaphor, Jesus identifies himself with the bread from heaven. This "living bread" gives life, indeed, eternal life. So part of our question is being answered.

What happens in the Eucharist? We are being fed—our deepest human needs are being met. But why don't we *feel* something, if that's the case? The important thing is not what we feel—it is what God is doing. We come to the Lord's Table—we come to Jesus—in search of that which will meet our deepest needs. There, at the Lord's Table, in the bread and wine, God meets us. We are in the presence of the Father and the Son, led by the Spirit. That's true, despite what we feel. If we do become aware of the presence of God in a new and deep way, we can receive that gift. Regardless of our feelings, God's act for us in Christ invites us to look, listen, and believe.

Then comes the word that draws us directly into our question: "The bread that I

Bible 301 ☐

Distribute copies of your church's Communion liturgy. Examine the prayers and Scriptures used. Invite your pastor to talk with you about "The Great Thanksgiving" portion of the liturgy. What is happening during this part of the sacrament?

give for the life of the world is my flesh" (verse 51). The word, *flesh*, is chosen deliberately. The Greek is *sarx*, the physical tissue of the body—muscle, skin, bone, and organs. In 1:14 we read that "the Word became flesh." The technical theological term for this is *Incarnation*, taken from two Latin words meaning, "in the flesh." At the heart of the faith, for this Gospel and the community for whom it was written, is a basic reality. In Jesus of Nazareth, the Divine Word, the Son of God became human. He took on human flesh, lived and died as a human being, and brought us life. The very fact of the Incarnation, of the Word coming into the world, is a gift of salvation for all the world. Verse 51 is clearly about Incarnation—and about the Eucharist. (And, as an important aside, verse 51 may very well be the most original form of Jesus' words establishing the sacrament.) In the Eucharist, the sign of God's incarnation in the Christ is re-presented to us.

They Still Don't Get It! ■

What is the emotional difference between hearing the minister say, "This is the body of Christ, broken for you," and Jesus' words that we must eat his flesh? What is the reality of which Jesus speaks?

They Still Don't Get It!

The crowd is shocked at the language about eating Jesus' flesh. People all through the ages have been shocked by it. Origen of Alexandria, the great biblical scholar and theologian (c. 185–c. 254) says, in *Contra Celsum*, vi 27, that the pagans were spreading all kinds of charges against the Christians for eating human flesh. This statement reflects a common charge in the Roman world—that Christians gathered to eat flesh, sometimes that of a child sacrificed on the altar. When I was in college, a senior biology major asked to speak in chapel. He used the occasion to charge that Christians were cannibals, because of the language about eating the body of the

Lord. To speak of Christ in the flesh is to witness to the reality of his humanity. In the first century, there was little argument over the divinity of Christ, but many disputed his humanity. It was essential to faith to confess that Jesus came in the flesh and that he was fully human.

The Third Discourse ■

Do you believe that, when we partake of the elements, we "take in" some of the qualities of Jesus the Christ? What do the statements in the text that Incarnation and Eucharist are linked and that we find new life through participation in the Eucharist mean for you?

The Third Discourse: John 6:53-59

Now come the explicit references to Eucharist—eating the flesh and drinking the blood of the Son of Man. If the crowd was shocked before, imagine how they felt now. If you don't eat the flesh and drink the blood, you don't have life. That certainly sounds like cannibalism—or, at least, like beliefs from older cultures that believed eating the flesh of an enemy would give you the strength and other qualities of that enemy. That second notion, in fact, does apply here. One of the things we believe about the Eucharist is that, when we eat and drink, we do "take in" some of the qualities of Jesus the Christ. Although bread and wine (or even grape juice) are not the literal, physical body and blood of Christ, Christ is present in the physical elements; in eating and drinking, we receive the spirit of Christ or the divine nature into our souls. St. Ignatius of Antioch, in about A.D. 115, said that the bread and wine of the Eucharist were the "medicine of immortality."

Let's remind ourselves of a couple of other points. First, the "flesh and blood" are clear affirmations of the Incarnation of the Son. He did not come in some kind of spiritual way, but as a real human being with real flesh and blood. Second, participating in the Eucharist—eating the flesh and drinking the blood of Christ—is closely linked to the gift of life. One of the ways we find new life in

Christ is through participation in the Eucharist. Not only is the Evangelist echoing Jesus' words, he is also making a strong statement to his own church, decades after the Resurrection. He is saying, "If you want to have new life in Christ, here is where you find it."

Eating the flesh and drinking the blood leads to the gift of eternal life. Clearly, we are not talking about a literal eating of Christ's flesh and a literal drinking of Christ's blood. But when we eat and drink the consecrated elements of bread and wine/grape juice, we participate in a mystery that leads to eternal life in the present and the promise of resurrection on the last day. John's understanding of eternal life operates on two levels. First, he understands that "seeing and believing" and participating in the Eucharist bring us to a new quality of life that participates in eternity, here and now. Second, he understands that the quality of eternal life that we experience now is a foretaste of the life of the Resurrection we will experience on the last day. The Eucharist is, somehow, the "medicine of immortality."

There are more clues to John's understanding of the Eucharist. Participation in the Eucharist draws us into a new relationship with Christ. This relationship is an extension of the relationship between the Father and the Son. We receive life from the sacrament because, in the sacrament, we share in the relationship of the Father and the Son—and this relationship gives us life. So what happens when we take Communion? The Gospel writer says we become a part of the relationship between the Father and the Son; we experience divine love in a direct and intimate way.

What is the relationship between the Eucharist and eternal life?

Put It All Together ■

Pull back and look at the "big picture" as the session draws to a close. Recall the "discourse pattern" and how it drove you deeper into the theology of the bread metaphor and the Eucharist. You explored the bread metaphor, along with some parallels, in the light of who Jesus is. Finally, you talked about the metaphor in terms of the Eucharist.

What have you learned? Who is Jesus? How is Christ present in the Eucharist? Who is welcome at the table?

Put It All Together

In John 6, we see the bread metaphor used in connection with the manna in the wilderness, the Incarnation of the Son, and the Word that gives and sustains life. Jesus transforms and fulfills all the metaphors when he says "I am the bread of life." The metaphors still carry their original meaning and context, but they are also redefined, on a deeper level, by the person of Jesus himself. What is the bread that gives life? It is not the manna— our ancestors ate that and died. It is not the loaves with which Jesus fed five thousand (or more) people—those people became hungry again. The true bread from heaven is Jesus, the Christ, the Son of God, who gives his flesh for the world.

All these metaphors are caught up in the Eucharist. We usually define Eucharist in terms of Jesus' death ("on the night when he was betrayed . . .") but it rightfully belongs to all of Jesus' life. That is why we call it Eucharist, which means "Thanksgiving." It is not a memorial feast of death, but a joyful feast of life. This bread (metaphor for Christ) gives life. So instead of long faces and solemn music, I sometimes think we should celebrate the Eucharist with a brass band, the choir singing "Hallelujah!" and dancing in the aisles. That's probably a bit much for most of our churches, so we'll settle for songs and smiles and joyful hearts. Eucharist marks our full participation in all of Jesus' life and gifts.

John's Gospel sees Eucharist, not as a memorial, but as a meal of presence. We eat *together with Christ* because Christ comes to join us at his table. Christ is present for us, as we are for him. It's not like sitting in a restaurant where many patrons have their cell phones glued to their ears. I always wonder: to whom are they present? In the

Eucharist, Christ is very present—and we come to make ourselves present to him.

This gives us a new way of looking at who is welcome at the table. We can't claim exclusive rights to Jesus' flesh and blood—they are given for all. So how can we exclude anyone who believes, even just a little, from the table? As a pastor, I scandalized several congregations by encouraging my toddler and pre-school-age children to participate in the Eucharist. People were scandalized that these children were participating, because how could these children understand anything about the service? I suspect they understood, far better than most adults, that the service was a mystery, but that it was a mystery about Jesus, and they wanted to be part of it. I tried to lead folk gently to see that we can't exclude children from Jesus' table. Later, when communion by intinction became a common practice, we used a common loaf. The children were delighted when given a large piece of the loaf. They seemed to know instinctively that this was a good thing, and therefore they needed a lot of a good thing!

Ultimately, it is the risen Christ who comes to us to make the sacrament real for us. Christ commands us not only to welcome all to his table, we are to invite all to come so that he may meet all for whom he died and lives again.

Close With Prayer

Gracious God, you have established the means of grace in which you come to us in your Son Jesus Christ that we may receive the gift of eternal life. We are overwhelmed that in the simple act of following Christ's command to remember him in the breaking of bread and sharing the cup, you become present with us and for us in saving power. Although we cannot explain how this becomes possible for us, we offer you thanks for the Bread of life that feeds our souls and gives us the assurance of eternal life in your presence. Amen.

Session Six

Banquet Parables

Session Focus ■

This session focuses on banquet parables, with an emphasis on how the parables relate to the idea of the "messianic banquet," the great feast day in the kingdom of God.

Session Objective ■

By participating in this session you will (1) explore stories about banquets and the kingdom of God; (2) explore table fellowship as a theme for the Kingdom; and (3) examine details that seem contradictory.

Session Preparation ■

Read this session carefully. Think about the kind of etiquette practiced at dinner parties (and elsewhere) in today's society. How do we use social occasions to seek power, influence, and self-promotion? Keep those examples in mind as you prepare to lead this session. You will find more than one occasion where they are appropriate.

Choose from among these activities and discussion starters to plan your lesson.

Remember when we had strict, though unwritten, social rules about dinner parties? If you were invited to someone's home for a meal, you were expected to invite him or her in return. The idea was to accept the invitations that made you "upwardly mobile" in the social scheme. If you accepted invitations from some people in the community, then you were no longer invited to the "best homes." Of course, pastors were mostly exempt from those rules. It was recognized that pastors had to accept dinner invitations from parishioners who were lower on the social scale. Mercifully, pastors were not expected to reciprocate every dinner invitation. Seems foolish, doesn't it? What difference does it make, anyway? Well, in other times, in some circles, it made a tremendous difference.

It's Where You Sit: Luke 14:7-14

Meals in first-century Palestine were more than just eating food. They were important social ceremonies. People noticed where one ate (Luke 5:29), with whom one ate (5:30), whether one washed before meals (7:44-46), and where one reclined to eat. All of this was determined by one's social position. (Just like some public banquets today, where the more important you are, the closer you sit to the head table.)

This passage in Luke contains two of

Meals in first-century Palestine were a bit like some office parties today. Where one reclined to eat was important, so were the persons with whom one ate, and so on. Ask group members to imagine a social gathering they attended recently. Was there maneuvering to be closer to powerful persons? What was the maneuvering like? What was the conversation about the maneuvering like?

Read Luke 14:7-14. What specific advice did Jesus give? How many rules of hospitality did Jesus break?

Jesus' parables about humility and table fellowship, both of them told at a formal dinner. Jesus told the first parable to the guests, who were jockeying for places of honor at the banquet. The sayings are almost more like a guide to "how to succeed without really trying," than a typical parable. Look at what Jesus says to the guests.

- Don't sit down in the place of honor. What if someone more important has been invited? You could be publicly embarrassed by being asked to take a lower seat—in fact, the lowest place.
- Instead, take the lowest place to begin with. Then the host may say, "Friend, move up higher"; and you will be honored instead of embarrassed.
- Then comes the Kingdom saying about those who exalt themselves being humbled, and vice versa.

Jesus is not to be confused with Miss Manners. Jesus is not the model guest. He "lectures" both the other guests, and the host. To the guests he says, "Don't set yourself up for embarrassment." In this saying, there is no middle ground. There is either shame or honor. Honor cannot be gained by grasping it for one's self. Honor is given to us by others.

Have you attended a company Christmas party and chuckled over the person who was hanging around the fringes of the group where the vice president stood? Remember the chuckles that went around your corner of the room at the way this person was trying to get the attention of the higher-ups and to gain the reputation of someone who could chat easily with them? That's a modern version of what Jesus is talking about.

But the saying is more than savvy career advancement advice that might appear in a business magazine. Jesus tells those who want honor to take the last place, what is called by some scholars "the least seat." This is the place at the banquet table where the youngest and least important of the group usually sat. The person in the "least seat" was expected to pour another round of wine, if servants were not present at the moment, and to perform other services for the other guests. That's the seat Jesus advises the glory-seekers to take. The Kingdom is a reverser of values! And it's all about where you sit!

It's About Whom You Invite

Whom do we invite to dinner? How do we build community around the table? How did Jesus suggest table fellowship could be profaned?

It's About Whom You Invite

Hosts, on the other hand, seem to need recognition as much as the guests. They invite people who will give them honor, who will help their standing in the community, and who will invite them in return. To them, Jesus says that the sense of community that is built around the table is too sacred to be profaned for private advantage. Persons should be invited for their own sake and not because of what they can do for us.

When I was senior pastor at a growing church, my wife and I developed a custom of inviting one couple from the congregation for dinner once a month. We spent a lot of time deciding whom to ask. The only criterion we applied was whether we'd like to get to know them better. Most of them did not have positions of power or prestige in the church; they were simply fascinating people. We did that for about two years, and the most wonderful thing about those evenings is that we developed friendships and community and discovered fascinating things about people we would otherwise never have known.

Jesus suggested inviting four specific groups of people. Who were they? Look at Leviticus 21:17-23 to see what Torah said about these groups of people. Then look carefully at the citation in the text about which people were denied entrance into the community at Qumran. How did the listeners respond to Jesus' advice?

Jesus says (verses 12-14) to the host at this banquet, be careful whom you invite. If you invite the usual folks, the ones who can invite you in return, or do you some big favor, what have you done? Have you sought the interests of the Kingdom or your own?

Then Jesus listed four groups of people who should be invited. Now these groups are not your basic key to getting ahead in the world. They are precisely the people who cannot help you:

- poor
- crippled
- lame
- blind

Contrast this guest list with the persons welcomed by the Qumran community:

"And let no person smitten with any human impurity whatever enter the Assembly of God. And every person smitten with these impurities, unfit to occupy a place in the midst of the Congregation, and every [person] smitten in his flesh, paralysed in his feet or hands, lame or blind or deaf, or dumb or smitten in his flesh with a blemish visible to the eye, or any aged person that totters and is unable to stand firm in the midst of the Congregation: let these persons not enter" (1QSa 2:3-8, quoted in *The New Interpreter's Bible*, Vol. IX; page 287).

There is a real contrast between the restrictions that human beings, even in the community of faith, put on community and the spirit of openness that Jesus displays. Jesus' openness, if we accept it for ourselves, frees us from the necessities of power and position and sets us free to create genuine community. Moreover, it allows us to do so in the security of God's grace.

The practice of humility in our hospitality is proper for Christian disciples. The Kingdom WILL turn our world upside down. In the Kingdom, there will no longer be any standards and practices of discrimination—even the outcasts will be accepted as equals. God does not look at the glamour and power on our guest list. What God looks for is this: Have we been generous and inclusive (living the Kingdom) in our daily social relationships?

Jesus had a reputation in some circles as a glutton and a drunkard. That may be because he enjoyed meals so much. He loved not just the food, but also the company. Jesus saw mealtime as a rich opportunity for creating bonds of love and community among persons. He practiced an inclusive community that was a promise of the kingdom of God.

When we "do lunch" with friends, not to conduct business, but to build relationships, we also build love and community. The same is true of the church. When we sit down at potlucks and picnics together, we build love and community. We have already seen (Session 2) that a major crisis for the early church was who ate with whom. Paul and Peter came to verbal blows over that issue (Galatians 2:11-14). There are barriers to community in all our churches today. Wouldn't it be ironic if the key to dealing with all barriers of exclusion was learning the proper table manners of the kingdom of God?

> If we were to practice Jesus' pattern for table fellowship, how might it affect the life in our church?

I Cannot Come to Your Banquet: Luke 14:15-24; Matthew 22:1-14

The two parables are similar, though the details are considerably different. Luke's host is a wealthy citizen; Matthew's is a king. That's because, at least in part, Luke tells a

I Cannot Come to Your Banquet ■

Read aloud these two passages. Listen to the presentations of the parable by the Gospel writers.

story about hospitality and reversals in the Kingdom. Matthew has given the story an allegorical interpretation, making it a rehearsal of God acting in history for salvation. We'll look first at the parable in Luke, then at the interpretation in Matthew.

Luke 14:15-24 ■

Read together Luke 14:15-24. Work out the narrative plot, and record it on the board. (This is simply reporting what came first, second, and so on.) Remember the backgound of hospitality and social customs, with all the implications the background brings to the story.

Luke 14:15-24

The parable assumes all the social customs and social stratification of a first-century Palestinian city. The host was a wealthy person, who could well afford to give a banquet. So he sent invitations to his dinner. Etiquette required two invitations. The first was sent well in advance. This invitation was acknowledged and accepted. The advance invitation allowed the guests to check around that the host had, indeed, made all the proper preparations for the feast and that the right people had been invited—*and* had accepted! There was some serious snobbery at work. The second invitation was delivered by the servants on the day of the banquet and was simply a courtesy reminder. Tonight is the night!

Immediately, the invited guests began to make excuses. We don't know if the host were suddenly the subject of a Roman investigation, and no one wanted to be seen with him; or if he had committed some serious social sin and been declared a pariah by the "in crowd." For whatever reason, the guests all made excuses. The excuses were thin and a snub. They remind us of the old story about the farmer who didn't want to lend a neighbor a rope because he might need it to tie up a pile of sand. When the neighbor protested that he couldn't do that with a rope, the farmer said, "You can do anything with a rope if you don't want to lend it." For the guests, who had decided to slight the invitation, any excuse was good enough. For example, who would buy land without checking it out first? or a new car without a test drive and some research?

Snubbed by his peers, the host turned to the only social groups available to him—he invited the very people social convention said he should not invite. Now these are the same people Jesus had just told the host he *should* invite. (Do we see a trend developing here?) When the host invited these people, he thumbed his nose at social standards. He insulted his peers and his family. From now on, he *would* be a social pariah, for he had dared to fly in the face of socially acceptable standards.

So the slaves went out and found the poor—but there was still room. The statement to "compel them to come in" has an interesting social background. The homeless lived outside the city walls; and the gates were shut in the evening, partly to keep these homeless persons from bothering the well-to-do. This social ostracism probably was enforced by the authorities, so the servant might very well have had to "compel" the homeless to come in where they were not allowed by law or custom.

The closing statement is telling. The ones who were invited and made lame excuses would have no part in the church. This is, in fact, the point of the story. Jesus was talking about the invitation to the Kingdom. There will be incredible reversals in the kingdom of God. Those who seemingly would surely be invited exclude themselves, and those who were unlikely to be invited will be included. Part of the criteria for exclusion/inclusion will be the response to table fellowship. In Matthew 25:31-48, Jesus says that one criterion for the Judgment will be hospitality—did you feed the hungry and otherwise help

What is Jesus saying about the Kingdom and the ways in which people respond to the Kingdom? What do all the "reversals" mean for the Kingdom?
Both this parable and Matthew 25:31-48 suggest that one criterion for the Judgment will be hospitality. Invite the participants to read Matthew 25:31-48 carefully. Ask: What are the differences in hospitality in the two parables? How does one qualify for the Kingdom in Matthew 25? in Luke 14:15-24?

to meet human need? Here, he says that one criterion will be, how open were you to table fellowship? Did you welcome the invitation to dinner?

Matthew 22:1-14 ◼

Read Matthew 22:1-14. Ask: How is this story different from the one we just read in Luke? List responses on chalkboard or on a piece of posterboard. Point out that a major difference is found in the way the two writers interpret the story. Luke tells a story to make a point; Matthew makes the story into an allegory about the messianic banquet. Point out what the text says about allegorical interpretation.

Matthew 22:1-14

Matthew provides an allegorical interpretation, in which the original dinner party has become the messianic banquet. (Allegory is a way of interpreting Scripture in which each element in the story comes to stand for something else.) The original parable was very close to what Luke says—it's a story that makes its own point. Matthew has added another level of interpretation of the story. Now the setting is not the original dinner party; it's about the kingdom of God. The dinner has become the messianic banquet (see below, pages 72–73).

The Kingdom is not compared to the king, but to the situation in which the king sends out invitations to a banquet. As we've seen, Luke treats the invitations as a straightforward story; Matthew makes the story into an allegory for God's invitation to all the world to come to salvation. The second invitation goes out, complete with a partial menu. And people refuse to come.

In Matthew's version of the parable, the invited guests don't make excuses. They simply go about their business and refuse to come. Or, in some cases, they actually mistreat the slaves who come with the invitation or even kill them. To refuse a king's invitation is the equivalent of rebellion. Since so many of them refused, this could look like a conspiracy, which would make the case for rebellion even stronger.

Examine the details of the allegory. For what does each character, or set of characters, in Matthew, represent?

Matthew then provides allegorical labels for the persons in the parable. The first group of slaves is like the prophets, who proclaimed God's word to Israel and were mistreated or even killed. God's invitation was ignored. The unfaithfulness of Israel and Judah led to their destruction. This is the point, at least for Matthew, of verse 7, with the reference to the king sending his army, killing these rebellious subjects, and destroying their city.

On the level of the parable, or in real life, this is not a realistic point. No king would wage war and destroy his own city, while his dinner cools and spoils! On the level of Matthew's allegory, it works perfectly fine. In fact, verse 7 may well be Matthew's reflection on the destruction of Jerusalem by the Roman armies. Christian historians, such as Eusebius, and the Jewish historian Josephus agree that one of the causes of that destruction was the murder of James the Just, who was considered a holy man and a prophet.

After the judgment, and the war, the banquet room is still empty. So the king sent out another group of slaves, with yet another invitation. The invitation was not restricted to a select list of guests. It was a universal invitation to all persons. Those who respond include both good and bad persons, just as Matthew found in his own church—and as we find in our churches.

Verses 11-13 are an addition to the original parable, and one of the hardest parts of the Gospels for us to understand. After all, everyone was invited. How could everyone who was pulled off the streets and dragged into the banquet hall be expected to wear the proper clothes? Indeed, given the universality of the invitation, why assume that many of the guests would even have access to the proper clothes? Yet, apparently, everyone does wear the proper clothes, except for one poor soul.

Why is one guest expelled from the party? What does the wedding feast represent?

Clearly this is not a realistic story; Matthew wants to make a theological point. And what is that point? Actually, it is difficult to know for certain. But, we know that, in early Christianity, baptism involved putting on a new set of clothes. Putting on those clothes was a metaphor for the new life, for "putting on Christ." So perhaps Matthew is talking about baptism, about "putting on Christ," and one person has come to the banquet without being in the proper relationship with Christ. Alternatively, it may refer to the righteous deeds of the saints (Revelation 19:8).

The man had no excuse, so he was cast out. The judgment was harsh; indeed, it seems to run counter to everything Jesus says about acceptance and inclusion. Matthew, however, is not thinking about a real wedding banquet, where we are expected to "make allowances." He is thinking about the Last Judgment, where those who have not responded to Christ are, indeed, excluded.

"Many are called, but few are chosen." Haven't we been hearing that the Kingdom is inclusive? What does this paradox tell us?

"For many are called, but few are chosen" (Matthew 22:14). The call is the invitation to become a disciple of Jesus. And all are invited to do that. Being "chosen," however, depends on showing real Christian faith in deeds of love and justice. God's grace calls everyone to the banquet of the Messiah; it is a universal and inclusive call. Some choose not to respond to the call. Some appear to answer the call but fail to live in righteousness. So it is true that not everyone makes it into the kingdom of God. The ones who don't make it, however, are self-selected. The church does not get to decide who will, and who won't, make it into heaven. All our rules and regulations are as nothing in the light of God's love and grace.

The question is not human rules but

response to God's grace. What did we do with the gift we were given? We'll be surprised at people who are included in the Kingdom, many of whom were systematically excluded by the church. And we'll be surprised, Matthew tells us, at people who are not in the Kingdom!

The Messianic Banquet

How does the table fellowship of the Eucharist reveal the nature of the kingdom of God?

Addendum—the Messianic Banquet

Jesus often used the metaphor of a great meal as a sign for the coming of the Kingdom. A technical term for that meal is the "messianic banquet," or the "banquet feast of the Messiah." This was a familiar metaphor for the Jews—Isaiah 25:6; 4 Ezra 6:51ff; 1 Enoch 62:14; 2 Baruch 25:5 all refer to the banquet of the Messiah. The messianic banquet is a metaphor for life in the kingdom of God. Jesus also refers to the many who will sit at table in the kingdom of God (Luke 13:29; Matthew 8:11). They will come from the four corners of the earth and feast with the patriarchs and the prophets. When the prodigal son returned home (Luke 15:11-24), his father threw a feast! There was eating, drinking, and dancing. In telling the story, Jesus implies that's what God is like. When you "come home," when you turn away from all the things you were pursuing instead of God and come home, God throws a party!

We do the same thing. I have a cousin I hadn't seen in years. We had kept in touch, and there was never any estrangement; we just hadn't seen each other in a long time. Recently we visited in my cousin's home. What a wonderful time! There was no big banquet, but the whole time we were there was like a party. We talked, we laughed, we wove new strands in our relationship. That's a faint echo of what happens when we come home to God. God throws a party! We call that party the messianic banquet.

Some folks refuse to participate in the party. The last part of the story of the prodigal son is about his older brother, who refused to go to the party because his feelings were hurt. The father made it clear that he had nothing but love for this older son, but they needed a party to welcome the younger one back home. The stories about a banquet in this session include the reminder that some people choose not to come. They have other things they want to do. They aren't willing to accept the openness and grace of the invitation. It may be that they don't want to associate with others who are invited.

That's one danger of becoming a Christian. We are called to be brothers and sisters of people we don't think are worthy of that relationship. Imagine, for a minute, all the people to whom we feel morally superior, for whatever reason. Now imagine the great banquet feast of the Messiah. It's a magnificent dinner party, filling the whole expanse of heaven. Seated in places of honor are some of the very people to whom we feel superior! Then you discover you aren't at the banquet at all: You're on the outside, looking in.

Close With Prayer ■

Gracious God, give us the grace, we pray, to respond joyfully to your invitation.

Give us the grace to be open to all the others who are invited to the banquet. Help us in humility to take our proper place and to worship you in the holy fellowship of all who respond to your invitation; in Jesus' name. Amen.

Session Seven

The Last Supper

Session Focus ■

This session focuses on the Last Supper of Jesus with his disciples, a special feast that celebrated freedom, salvation, and God's mighty acts in history.

Session Objective ■

Persons will explore connections between Jesus' last meal with his followers and the sacrament of Holy Communion in the church today. They will discover how John's Gospel emphasizes table fellowship as a key to community.

Session Preparation ■

If you choose to model a *triclinium*, you'll need a low (18" to 24") coffee table and at least two cushions from deck lounges.

If you decide to have a foot-washing service, you will need a basin, water, and towels. Tell the group ahead of time that you will have this service as a part of the session, and invite persons to decide whether they want to participate.

You will need a Bible dictionary to use for an activity in this session.

The importance of the Last Supper as a part of the story of Jesus' suffering, death, and resurrection has been dealt with in another book in this series (*The Passion and Death of Jesus*). We will touch only briefly on the ties between the meal and salvation here and focus on the meal itself. Meals were important to Jesus, and Luke tells us that Jesus was eager to share this last meal with his closest friends (Luke 22:15). In our study of the meal, we will look first at the accounts in the Synoptic Gospels (Matthew, Mark, and Luke), then at the entirely different account in John's Gospel, and finally at Paul's account in First Corinthians.

The Last Supper in the Synoptic Gospels: Matthew 26:17-29; Mark 14:12-25; Luke 22:7-20

The Synoptic Gospels all agree that Jesus' last meal was the Passover Seder. For the Jews of Jesus' day, as in our own day, the Passover was a celebration of freedom. It celebrated the night when God's angel of death "passed over" the homes of the Hebrews in Egypt and caused Pharaoh to allow Moses to lead them out of slavery. They were convinced that God was in the Exodus, bringing God's people into a new relationship and creating both a nation and a faith. Passover was a feast of thanksgiving, a memory of God's mighty acts in history, an awareness of

Choose from among these activities and discussion starters to plan your lesson.

Model the Setting ■

If you have space at all, create a model of the way in which Jesus and the disciples ate what we call the Last Supper.

If you can find a low (18" to 24") coffee table, put it in the center of the room. Place on one side of it cushions taken from deck lounges. Place the cushions with the short end at a 45-degree angle to the table. Put a small plate of fruit, two plates, two cups, and perhaps some bread or cheese on the table. Invite two volunteers to recline on the cushions, on their left elbows. This will put one person with her or his back to the other and with her or his head about chest level with the other person.

Explain that this would have been the way Jesus and the disciples ate the Passover, and the model will be particularly important when you look at the story in John's Gospel.

The Last Supper in the ■ Synoptic Gospels

Point out the background on the Passover as a celebration of freedom. Then ask: What persons other than the Twelve were probably present at the Last Supper?

God's presence in their lives, and the establishment of God's reign on earth. In the context of the meal, God's mighty acts for Israel were rehearsed, and there was instruction on how God's people were to live in response to their freedom/salvation. It was in that context that Jesus and his followers gathered. The Synoptics tell us they did not gather as a family group, which was the common custom, but rather as a teacher and his disciples. Some scholars, however, do raise the possibility that there may have been more than just the Twelve with Jesus at the supper and that at least some family members were present.

In any case, Jesus saw to it that all the proper preparations for the Passover were made. These preparations included

- finding a place inside the walls of Jerusalem (the only proper place to celebrate);
- searching the room for yeast, and removing any items that might contain yeast;
- securing a lamb and having it ritually slaughtered by the priests;
- roasting the lamb and preparing the other necessary items.

Jesus himself, apparently, knew of the place. He sent the disciples into the city to meet a man carrying a jar of water (Mark and Luke), who would lead them to the room. Because carrying water was "woman's work" in the first century, a man carrying water would be unusual enough to serve as a reliable guide.

All of the disciples went to prepare for the feast (in contrast to John, who has only Peter and the beloved disciple perform this task).

When they came for the meal, they

Form three teams. Ask one team to read Matthew 26:17-29, the second to read Mark 14:12-25, and the third to read Luke 22:7-20.

Ask the team that read Mark to put the narrative plot in a column down the center of the chalkboard or piece of poster paper. (Remember that the narrative plot is a listing of all events in the sequence in which they occurred.) Then ask the teams that read Matthew and Luke to write, in the two outside columns, all the material in their accounts that are different from Mark. After looking at how Matthew and Luke are different from Mark, ask: How different are Matthew and Luke from each other?

reclined at the table. The tables were set in a large *U*-shape, or *triclinium*, with cushions all the way around the outside. The inside was left free, so the household servants could offer food and drink. Short couches were placed so that one end of the couch reached the low banquet table. Diners reclined on their left elbow and ate with their right hand. Because the couches were short, the diners' feet and lower legs stuck out past the end of the couch. (This is important for helping us understand John's account of Jesus washing the disciples' feet.) Usually the couches were broad enough for two persons to recline together. They were placed at a slight angle to the table. They reclined because Passover is a celebration of freedom and, at Passover, all Jews are free.

The meal itself was undoubtedly a Seder celebration. The few details we have of the meal all suggest that. However, we don't have any written accounts of the Seder ritual before the second century, and we don't know how much of first-century practices those accounts reflect. Eating can create a community among those who share the food. Throughout Jesus' ministry he ate with "sinners" and outcasts, showing his solidarity with, and commitment to, them. On that night in Jerusalem, Jesus began a new community, one rooted in his own life, teachings, death, and resurrection. When we partake of the Lord's Supper, we become a part of that community. When we celebrate with open hearts, we are called to open ourselves to the outcasts of our society and welcome them into our community. When a pastor says, "All are welcome," we are reminded that we are not to put barriers in the way of those whom Jesus has called into fellowship with himself.

Consider how the Lord's Supper is celebrated in our churches today. Invite discussion on how the Lord's Supper creates community. When we say, "all are welcome," what are the risks we take?

What does the Lord's Supper say to you about creating community with followers of the Jewish faith in your city or town?

How does the Lord's Supper create community among believers? Invite persons in the group to tell stories about how the sacrament has broken down barriers and created community for them.

The Lord's Supper also creates community with the Jewish people. This interfaith community is one of mutual respect and understanding. When we celebrate the Lord's Supper, we embrace God's saving act in the Exodus from Egypt. When we eat the bread and drink the cup, we say that the God we worship is also the God who is committed to the salvation of the people of Israel.

The Lord's Supper creates community with other believers. In traditions where Christians go to the communion rail to receive the elements, it is literally true that we cannot come close to Christ without physically coming closer to one another. The liturgy invites us to exchange signs of reconciliation and peace. I was once at a clergy retreat. Also present was a fellow clergyperson, with whom I had been involved in a massive dispute before and during the annual conference session. All of us present were uneasy about how our relationship might work itself out, especially if we had to work closely together. When we came to the time for exchanging signs of peace, he and I started toward each other. He pulled me into his arms and, with tears streaming down his cheeks, he said, "I'd like for us to take Communion together." The Lord's Supper invites us into deep community with other believers.

Finally, the Lord's Supper creates a community with the Lord. It is the Lord's Table, and all the rules of table fellowship about which we've read in this book apply. Jesus Christ is the host, and bids us welcome. We have only to respond in thanksgiving. Many persons say they "don't feel anything" when they partake of the Supper. Feeling is good, but it is not a prerequisite. Christ is present in our lives anyway, no matter what we feel or don't feel.

Some say they don't like Communion for a variety of reasons. All those reasons ignore the reality of fellowship at the meal. What is important is *not* the method of Communion, or how much extra time it adds to the service, or anything else. What *is* important is that Jesus Christ welcomes us to the table and offers us fellowship with himself as we eat there.

Several meanings emerge from an examination of the Lord's Supper in the Synoptics. Matthew relates the Lord's Supper to the forgiveness of sins, which he sees as Jesus' primary mission. Matthew understands forgiveness in terms of Jesus' death as the sacrifice that creates a covenant between God and people. Historically, many Christians have lived out this understanding of Communion; and it has been a solemn time, with a heavy emphasis on repentance and forgiveness. Until recently, the words of invitation in the ritual of The United Methodist Church put a heavy emphasis on repentance and new beginnings. Yet, eating together is more about table fellowship and the sharing of life. The meal invites us to remember all the meals that Jesus ate and all the meals that we have eaten. "Whenever you eat the bread, remember me." We are invited particularly to remember all who are outcasts of society.

The meal also involves the anticipation of the messianic banquet (see Session Six). Jesus' words that he would not drink the fruit of the vine until he drank it new in the Kingdom is a word of eschatalogical hope. So the Lord's Supper is also a promise of God's final victory over sin, death, and the Devil, and the establishment of the Kingdom in all its glory. The Lord's Supper is about the future, as well as about the past. Paul says much the same thing to the Corinthians:

What are the various interpretations given to the Eucharist? For instance, Matthew thinks it is about forgiving sins. The text suggests it is about fellowship, memory, and hope. What other meanings are possible?

Bible 301 ☐

Look up eschatology /eschatological *in a Bible dictionary. How does this meal offer hope for the future? What is the eschatological language used in "The Great Thanksgiving" (from the Holy Communion liturgy)?*

"For as often as you eat this bread and drink the cup, you proclaim the Lord's death until he comes" (1 Corinthians 11:26, see pages 82–85).

The Last Supper in John's Gospel: John 13:1-38

The Last Supper in John's Gospel ■

Invite persons to read John 13:1-38. Ask: What are the themes that are unique to John? (Remind group members to include the material about the Eucharist from John 6. See Session Five, pages 55–57.

How is table fellowship expressed by John?

In John's Gospel, we enter a world completely different from that of the Synoptics. For his own theological reasons, the writer of John does not place the institution of the Eucharist in the context of the Passover Seder, but in the great discourse following the feeding of the five thousand (see John 6 in Session Five, pages 55–57). At the Last Supper, John presents four separate elements, all closely woven together in one narrative:

- the foot washing: John 13:1-11;
- the discourse on service: John 13:12-20;
- the prophecy of betrayal: John 13:21-30;
- the new commandment and prophecy of denial: John 13:31-38.

All four elements are important for the Johannine theological scheme. We will examine all four, with primary emphasis on the first two elements: the foot washing and the discourse on service.

John is clear that the feast is somehow associated with the Passover, though not the Passover feast itself. In John's account, Jesus dies as the Passover lambs are being killed—a key theological statement that may or may not reflect historical reality. Certainly it disagrees with the Synoptics, who tell us that the Last Supper was the Passover meal. Some scholars have suggested that Jesus knew he was going to die and arranged to celebrate the feast early. Others have sug-

Talk about the foot washing. Remind participants again that lying on cushions meant the disciples' feet were in a position where Jesus could easily wash them. Invite persons to participate in a service of foot washing. To do this easily, you will need a large washbasin, a pitcher of (relatively) warm water, a minimum of two towels, and persons who are willing to participate. Place a towel on the floor, with the basin of warm water on one end of the towel. Next to the other end, place a chair where participants can sit. You, or another leader, kneel on the floor by the chair and basin. Invite persons to come to the chair barefoot. When a person sits in the chair, lift a foot, hold it over the basin, cup water in your other hand, and pour it over the foot. Repeat with the other foot. Then gently dry the person's feet with the towel. A particularly powerful moment could occur when a participant asks to change places with you and wash your feet. Be open for this possibility.

gested that Jesus observed the Essene calendar, which celebrated Passover on a different date than that established by the Temple authorities. Either scenario is certainly possible, but neither makes allowance for having the lamb ritually slaughtered by the priests— at the proper moment. However, the Essenes likely had a method for the slaughter of the lambs without taking them to the Temple. This would make the scenario presented in John's Gospel more plausible.

As we have seen earlier in this book, one of the common acts of hospitality was to provide water for washing the feet of dinner guests. Guests walked on dusty streets wearing open sandals, so their feet were dusty by the time they arrived. A basin of water and a towel were ready to welcome them and allow them to wash the dust from their feet. (They then went barefoot into the house.) In some cases, a servant was stationed at the entrance with basin and towel, ready to perform this service for the guests; in other cases, the guests washed their own feet.

However, the dinner didn't go right. In the first place, no one had made arrangements for water to wash their feet. In the second place, there was some discord about the seating. We can imagine it went something like this: Jesus invited the beloved disciple to recline at his right hand. We know that for certain, because John tells us (13:25) that the beloved disciple leaned "on Jesus' breast." That is, when they were reclining at table, his head was about even with Jesus' chest.

When Simon Peter heard that the beloved disciple was going to be on Jesus' right hand, he immediately assumed he would be on the left. After all, they had been the ones chosen to prepare the meal—it was only fitting that they have the seats of honor. Then he heard Judas (we presume) invited to sit at Jesus' left hand.

Perhaps Peter went all the way around the table to the "least seat," on the opposite wing of the *triclinium* from Jesus. (The seat of honor was not in the middle of the head table—the "bottom" of the U-shaped arrangement, as we would have it. Instead, it was at the very end of the right-hand upright of the U.) The "least seat" was for the youngest and least important member of the party.

Teach by Doing ■

We have been taught to interpret biblical texts on a literal basis as the most reliable way of getting at the "real" meaning. In the first centuries, the allegorical meaning of the text was more valued. Why do you think many prefer a literal interpretation?

Teach by Doing

Jesus took off his robe, gathered the basin and towel, and began to wash the feet of his disciples. Remember, because they were reclining on short couches, their feet were readily available, hanging over the ends of the couches. None of this crawling around under the table that I used to imagine, or asking the disciples to turn their chairs around! Note first that Jesus could do this because he was secure with his own identity. He knew that he came from God and was going to God, so he had no false pride about performing the tasks of a servant. In Jesus' table fellowship, he was free to be host and servant.

Peter protested against Jesus washing his feet for more than one reason. On one level, he was embarrassed. Perhaps Peter should have been washing the feet. On another level, he was embarrassed because he knew that Jesus was God's Son, and that status meant he should not be about the business of washing feet. Jesus was secure with his person and thus free to be a servant.

Jesus' response (verse 10) to Peter's protest may also be read on more than one level. It could mean simply that those who had bathed did not need to wash all over, but only rinse the dust from their feet. Or, it could be a reference to Judas's betrayal and mean that all of the disciples were clean except the one who would betray him. Or, it could be an indirect reference to baptism, with a parallel to the statement about bathing.

After washing their feet, Jesus spoke about service and about greatness, which probably made Peter squirm a bit. Jesus commanded his disciples to wash one another's feet. Now here is an interesting point. The common Protestant definition of a sacrament is something that Jesus initiated: a physical element of creation was used and there was a command by Jesus to observe the act. That being the case, foot washing appears to have the essential element of a sacrament. Perhaps as the Christian movement spread beyond Palestine, foot washing did not have meaning elsewhere; and thus it fell into disuse among most churches.

Another point about the meal itself. When the beloved disciple asked Jesus who would betray him (verse 25), Jesus replied that it would be the one to whom he gave the bread after he dipped it. At a time when people used bread as we use spoons, dipping the bread in dishes of food would be an ordinary part of the meal. The Synoptics say that Jesus' reply was "one who is dipping into the dish with me," that is, one who was seated close enough to use the same dish. This report heightens the sense of betrayal. Jesus and Judas shared bread together, and Judas left the table to gather Jesus' enemies to destroy him.

For worship resources related to foot washing, refer to *The United Methodist Book of Worship,* 351, or to the *Book of Common Prayer,* 274.

The Last Supper According to Paul ∎

What practices in the Corinthian church, in Paul's judgment, violated Jesus' practice of table fellowship? What were the

The Last Supper According to Paul: 1 Corinthians 11:17-34

Paul's reference to the Last Supper is the only account we have in Scripture, outside the Gospels. Let's set the stage for what Paul has to say. The early church celebrated the consequences of these violations on the Christian community? Invite the group to read 1 Corinthians 11:17-34.

Eucharist in the context of a full meal. When the community gathered, it was for a meal, during which bread was blessed and broken, and the cup was blessed and drunk. Remember we said earlier that eating together provides an opportunity for community and intimacy. We experience those when we go to church potlucks, pancake breakfasts, or carry-in suppers.

Recently my wife and I went to annual conference for the day. We sat down at lunch with a table full of strangers, only one of whom we had ever seen before. Soon conversation flowed freely as we ate, and we created a brief moment of intimacy and community. When we meet an old friend for lunch, or go out for dinner with friends, the community and intimacy that already exists between us is strengthened and renewed as we eat and talk together. The Corinthians were supposed to use their common meals as occasions for building community and intimacy across social barriers. Instead, Paul heard, there wee serious abuses of the practice of the common meal.

Early in the 1900's, US Protestants abandoned the common cup in favor of individual Communion glasses. How does this action tend to deny the words we use in the liturgy? What message is remembered best: what is said or what is done?

Apparently there were some members of the community who were wealthy, or at least comfortably well off. They came early and shared their food with "folks like them." They ate well and indulged in wine to the point where some even became drunk. Now this was a common practice at Roman banquets, where being drunk and satiated with food was a sign of politeness to the host.

Paul's concern was that there also were poor members of the church, some of them even slaves. They may have spent a long day working and have come to the dinner late, with only the little crusts of bread and sour wine they had been able to find. Paul was furious about the flagrant violation of table fellowship and Christian community. It was as bad as what he experienced at Antioch (Galatians 2), but also worse in some ways, because this was the Eucharist.

The ones who overindulged when others went hungry showed contempt for the church; that is, they were contemptuous of the meaning of community and intimacy created when all share together. Paul declared that their actions humiliated the poor. Paul fought with the Corinthians on the same front where he fought with Peter and Barnabas at Antioch—their desire to go back to the old, comfortable ways of living out cultural differences, instead of living in the strange, radical, newness of the life in Christ. The supper, Paul asserts, calls us to break down cultural and social barriers and create community with those who are different.

In the context of his argument about community, Paul reminded the Corinthians of the words of institution for the Lord's Supper. Paul also discussed sharing the sacrament in an "unworthy manner" (verses 27-34). There are some scary words here, and one does not treat them lightly. What does it mean to eat and drink in an unworthy manner?

Experience Beyond Physical Senses ■

What is meant by the term "eating in an unworthy manner"? If unworthy eating involves failing to "discern the Lord's body," how is the body discerned?

Experience Beyond Physical Senses

First, Paul says (verse 29), it means eating without discerning the body. On one level, this statement could mean the physical body of Christ, represented by the bread. If we eat without discerning Christ's presence, we eat unworthily. (Could this be a reason why some persons don't want to "take Communion," because they don't "feel" anything?) The more likely meaning of these words, given Paul's theology of the church, is that discerning the body refers to the church itself. To act like gluttons and ignore the hunger of others in the community is failing to discern the body.

Paul claims it is impossible to partake of the Eucharist in a "worthy" manner while completely ignoring the needs of others, particularly those who are brothers and sisters in Christ. It's not what we do to the elements that matters—it's what we do to the community. Whenever we eat the bread and drink the cup, we proclaim the Lord. Whenever we eat the bread and drink the cup and humiliate, neglect, or exclude others, we ignore the Lord in the very act of our proclaiming him. Our actions have become incongruent with our words.

Close With Prayer

Sing or read the following prayer:

"O the depth of love divine, the unfathomable grace! Who shall say how bread and wine God into us conveys! How the bread his flesh imparts, how the wine transmits his blood, fills his faithful people's hearts with all the life of God!

"Sure and real is the grace, the manner be unknown; only meet us in thy ways and perfect us in one. Let us taste the heavenly powers, Lord, we ask for nothing more. Thine to bless, 'tis only ours to wonder and adore."

—Charles Wesley
The United Methodist Hymnal, 627

Session Eight

Meals of Revelation and Reconciliation

Session Focus ■

This session focuses on meals as moments of revelation, when disciples come to a new understanding of Jesus, and moments of reconciliation, times when the estranged are restored.

Session Objective ■

You will explore how meals are moments of revelation and reconciliation. You will also explore the relationships between revelation, reconciliation, and the call to mission.

Session Preparation ■

You may want to ask the pastor or a member or members of the congregation who have been to the Holy Land to meet with your group, show pictures of the church that commemorates Jesus' breakfast with the disciples, and talk about what it meant to them. Or, you may want to arrange for the group to prepare and eat breakfast together, conducting the session around the tables.

You will need a Bible dictionary.

Meals are important to us. When we get together with family or friends, one of the things we consider is what we will serve for dinner, or where we will go to eat. When we have been estranged from someone, we work on the process of reconciliation by sharing a meal. Remember, in the ancient world, meals were occasions for "burying the hatchet," for creating community, for ensuring one another of protection and safety. Several of the Resurrection stories in the Gospels center around meals. In this session, we will examine the meals in Resurrection stories and see how the meals function as instruments of both revelation and reconciliation for the disciples and serve as models for the contemporary church.

Known in the Breaking of the Bread: Luke 24:13-35

The basic story is simple. Cleopas and an unnamed disciple were walking from Jerusalem to Emmaus, trying to deal with the heartbreak of Jesus' crucifixion and the strange reports they had heard from some of the women disciples that Jesus was alive. Cleopas and his companion belonged to the fellowship of Jesus' disciples in Jerusalem, which would also have included Mary, Martha, and Lazarus of Bethany, and proba-

Choose from among these activities and discussion starters to plan your lesson.

Known in the Breaking of the Bread

Ask persons to identify some of the elements of table fellowship present in the text.

Look together at Genesis 19:2-3 to see how the elements of table fellowship worked out between Lot and those strangers.

bly Joseph of Arimathea, and possibly Nicodemus from the Sanhedrin.

The Gospel writer uses the literary device of permitting the reader to know a truth unknown to the characters in the story. That is, we know the identity of the stranger who joined them on their walk and engaged them in conversation.

When they arrived in Emmaus Jesus walked ahead, as if continuing his journey. This is a tactful gesture on his part. He would not impose on the disciples or make them feel they had to offer him food or lodging. In Near Eastern cultures, it was proper etiquette for invited guests to turn down several invitations, requiring the host to press on them his hospitality. This was a face-saving gesture for all involved. If the invitation were only an empty formality, no one was put out by the refusal. If it were sincere, the sincerity would be made clear in the repetition.

Genesis 19:2-3, the story of Lot offering hospitality to the angels in Sodom, is an excellent example of how this social convention worked. The angels went home with Lot only after he "urged them strongly" (19:3). That's on the social level. On a theological level, this story reminds us that God never forces us to accept the divine presence into our lives. We are free to welcome or ignore God, just as we choose. Faith and any relationship with God are always a voluntary response to grace. At their urging, Jesus did accept their hospitality, putting into practice what he told his disciples in Luke 10:7 (see Session One) about accepting the hospitality of those who invite them into their homes.

There is that awkward moment when they sit down. Who will bless the food? We experience that at times, when a group is eating together or when we're in a restaurant with friends. Jesus quickly dealt with the awkwardness by taking charge of the meal, so that the guest became the host.

The meal itself is what scholars in literature call a recognition scene. At a dramatic moment in a story or play, something happens that causes someone to recognize the mysterious stranger. There are moments like this, for example, in the *Odyssey*, when the old servant recognizes Ulysses, or in *Ivanhoe*, when the mysterious knight is recognized as King Richard Coeur-de-Lion. Up to this point, the disciples had been blind as to Jesus' identity. He was merely a stranger who walked along the road with them. When they sat down for the meal, Jesus' actions led them to recognize him.

The verbs in verse 30 (*took, blessed, broke, gave*) are Jesus' signature actions. It's what he did at the feeding of the five thousand. It's what he did at the Last Supper. The disciples recognized the actions and immediately became aware that it was Jesus!

The supper at Emmaus is described in liturgical language (verse 30), but that does not mean that what happened was a Eucharist; rather it means that table fellowship can make any meal a sacred occasion. We've all known that reality.

Several months ago, I returned to a city where I had lived for some thirteen years. The one day we were there, I met an old friend and colleague for lunch. We were, and still are, close friends. Over lunch, we talked about what had happened in our lives since we were together last. A lot of what we talked about involved loss and pain. In the conversation, we revealed to each other a great deal about who we are at deep levels. We built, in that seventy-five minutes over

Invite participants to engage in a guided meditation. Ask everyone to find a comfortable and relaxed sitting position, to close their eyes, and to imagine the biblical scenes. Then say, "You are walking along a gravel road, through rolling hills, in early spring. (*Allow some silence, so they can begin to picture the scene in their minds.*) A friend is with you. You have just been in Jerusalem. What should have been one of the most exciting experiences of your life was ruined. Your leader was captured by the Romans and executed as a traitor. You are incredibly sad and you and your friend are talking about your feelings. (*Pause.*)

"A stranger, who is also walking the same way, catches up with you. After some greetings and remarks on the weather, he suggests that you seem sad and asks what's wrong. What will you tell him? (*Pause.*)

"After he listens to your outpouring of grief, he begins to talk about the Scripture, about how the Messiah was destined to die. What does he say to you? (*Pause.*).

"After a long walk, you reach home, and invite the stranger to stay for dinner. You sit down, he takes the bread and blesses it, then breaks it and gives it to you. What happens to you next?" (*Pause.*)

Tell the group members to open their eyes and come back to the present. Ask: How was it? What did you see? hear? experience? When Jesus talked to you about the Scripture, what did he say?

lunch, a much stronger level of intimacy and caring than we had before. Something sacred had taken place in our time together.

Cleopas and the other disciple experienced the presence of Christ at supper. My friend and I discovered that presence at lunch. The church experiences the presence of Christ when we gather at the Lord's Table. The sacrament is one of those places, as Dwight Vogel says, where God meets us "by previous appointment" (from *By Water and the Spirit*; Graded Press, 1993). Isn't that a wonderful phrase—"by previous appointment"? It means that we can always count on God being present, because God has chosen that place and that activity to be present. It is as if we have an unbreakable appointment, one on which we can always depend.

What happened in this story? Jesus opened the Scripture to his disciples; then he opened their eyes. The meal became a moment of revelation, when they recognized the Lord for who he was. And when they became aware that, all the time, he had been talking to them about Scripture, he had been opening their hearts to a deeper truth about the teachings found there.

Teaching and eating were (and are) partners in the revelation of the risen Lord. Cleopas and his companion recognized the Lord in the midst of an act of table fellowship, when they shared their bread with a stranger. I wonder what that suggests for ways in which we might find the Lord?

When we lived in Nashville, Tennessee, the church we attended offered hospitality to homeless men each Saturday evening during the winter months. We provided a hot dinner, showers, beds, an opportunity to wash clothes, and a hot breakfast on Sunday morning. Several times I agreed to help with this "Room in the Inn" on a particular evening my goal was to serve in the kitchen. I am an extreme introvert and find it hard to enter into conversation with strangers. That, however, was not to be. The "rules" were that we all sat down at table with our guests and talked with them. That is, of course, far better hospitality than lurking in the kitchen, no matter how comfortable the latter might be. I found, to my surprise, that I was able to talk with these homeless men and to develop some small sense of community out of our eating together. And I discovered that I saw Jesus Christ in the faces of those men.

Is There Anything to Eat?
Luke 24:36-43

Is There Anything to Eat? ▮

What happens in this story? What evidence of the Resurrection do we see?

Cleopas and his companion went running back to Jerusalem and told their story to the disciples gathered there, who, it turns out, had their own exciting story to tell. While they were talking and celebrating, Jesus himself appeared to them, and they were terrified. Good reaction! Luke seems to be aware that the common human reaction to a revelation of the divine is, in fact, terror.

In spite of all they were celebrating about the Resurrection, they were not prepared for Christ's appearance and thought they were seeing a ghost or a demon, who had come to trick them. So Christ offered them evidence of his resurrection.

Bible 301 ☐

Look up resurrection *in a Bible dictionary. What do you believe about the Resurrection?*

First, he showed them his hands and feet. Since the wounds are not mentioned, this is probably only a reference to the parts of his body that could be seen outside his clothing. What does this mean? Theologically, the action is a statement about the resurrection of the body, a key doctrine for the early church. Against those who argued that Jesus was not truly human, or that the Resurrection was only spiritual, they held that Jesus was not a disembodied spirit, but a whole person, body and spirit. For the disciples that first Easter, and for the church for whom Luke wrote his Gospel, this was a strong statement about the real presence of Christ.

The second proof was that Jesus asked for something to eat. This is a fascinating story about table fellowship. There wasn't much food around, but they found a piece of broiled fish and he ate that. This, again, is a reminder that the risen Christ was body and spirit. It is also about fellowship. Eating the food in their presence was an act of table fellowship that reminded the disciples they were safe, because they could eat together.

However they may have felt about their own failures and betrayal of Jesus, they did not need to fear his anger and retribution. They had eaten together and were reconciled.

So this meal is about revelation. The revelation was that Christ was risen from the dead—risen in the body and not just in spirit. It just might also be about something else as well. Some scholars suggest that these were meals of forgiveness. The disciples had all deserted Jesus when he was arrested and had to be feeling the guilt and pain of that desertion. Imagine their fear when they saw what they believed was a specter. When they realized it was Jesus, they were overjoyed. They knew he came in love and not in revenge. Eating together was a sign that they were forgiven, that the forgiveness had, in fact, already taken place. The meal was also about reconciliation, about putting the past behind them and moving into the future in a new relationship.

Why do you think Jesus asked for something to eat? What does that suggest about the nature of the Resurrection? What does it suggest about the relationship between Jesus and the disciples at that moment? What does their joy suggest about the character of Jesus?

What was revealed to the disciples at table with Christ? How does this narrative relate to your experience of the Lord's Table?

Feed My Sheep

If anyone in your group has been to the Holy Land (or if the pastor or someone else in the congregation has been), ask them to bring pictures of the little church that commemorates the breakfast by the Lake of Galilee and to tell about what visiting that site was like for them. If you can get reports from more than one person, so much the better. This should be a time for personal witness and reflection.

If you do not know of anyone in your community who has been to the Holy Land, consider the following alternative: as your group arrives, have breakfast in the final stages of preparation (and then reverse the order of the session, so this story comes first).
OR
Arrange to have a common breakfast in the church kitchen or fellowship hall, and conduct the session around the breakfast table.

What is the narrative plot here? What happens? List the responses on chalkboard or on posterpaper so you have an outline of the story. Then ask: Where are the moments of recognition in the story? Who are the people involved? How is recognition like a revela-

Feed My Sheep! John 21:1-19

On our last trip to Israel, the guide took our group outside a church on the shore of the Lake of Galilee and suggested that this *may* have been the place where the risen Christ prepared the breakfast for his disciples. Or, he said, it could have been in several other places; but, wherever it was, it was a place like this. Being from Missouri, I'm a natural skeptic, but I was more than willing to accept the possibility that the breakfast happened near here and that I could reflect on its meaning with joy. I suspect the disciples had some of the same mixed feelings of skepticism and joy that I had.

The central concept in the story of the breakfast is first about recognition/revelation, just as the Emmaus story is. The stranger told the fishermen to try a different spot. Dedicated fishermen are always ready to try one more spot, just in case. In this case, the stranger knew where the fish were. What a catch! While they were hauling in the nets, I imagine, the beloved disciple said, half to himself, "That's the Lord!" Recognitions and revelations often happen that way. We think we're doing something else, and the truth of what is really happening reaches up and hits us between the eyes. What happened next is so typical. The beloved disciple recognizes; Peter acts impetuously.

When the disciples reached the shore, they discovered that the Lord had prepared a meal for them. A charcoal fire was used to bake bread. Since an oven is not mentioned, the bread is likely to have been baked on some heated, flat rocks that would have been plentiful along the lakeshore. The bread would have been a flat bread, similar to contemporary pocket bread or pitah. A traditional means of broiling fish in Galilee is to encase the entire

Lion? What memories of other meals would they have had?

fish in moist clay. The clay-encased fish is then laid on the hot coals to bake. When the clay cracks, the fish is done. The clay is broken from the fish and the skin and scales adhere to the clay. The perfectly baked, succulent flesh of the fish can be easily removed from the bones. Clay deposits still exist on the shore of Lake Galilee near the site where tradition places this meal Jesus shared with his disciples.

When Jesus invited the disciples to come and eat, the bread and some fish were already baked. Then he prepared some seconds with the fish the disciples had just caught. In this narrative, the sign of grace is not the miraculous multiplication of 5 small fish into enough food to feed a multitude of five thousand; rather, there is an abundant provision of 153 fish. This large catch of fish was provided at Christ's direction following a long night of fruitless toil. Both feedings preserve a similar theme. In our want, God abundantly provides for our need. Christ spreads a table at which all are fed and all are satisfied. There is more than we can eat.

Near this site, Jesus had fed more than five thousand people with bread and fish. That event had to be in the minds of the disciples. Jesus revealed himself as the source of life in the feeding of the five thousand (see Session Five). Here, once again, he offered life to the disciples. The writer of John doesn't give any details about the meal, but we can be sure that Christ took the bread, blessed it, broke it, and gave it to them.

Having fed Peter, Jesus commanded Peter to feed others. The meaning of being at table with Christ is that his presence with us provides the paradigm for our life with others. He does not ask of us what he does not first provide to us. We can recall that on the night Jesus was betrayed, Peter took a sword and cut off the ear of Malchus (John 18:10). Jesus had been Peter's host at the Seder meal they had just eaten together. It was the duty of the host to protect his guest even after the meal. So Jesus acted quickly. He told Peter to put away his sword. This smart move prevented Peter's arrest for attempted murder. Having saved Peter from certain death at the hands of no-nonsense soldiers, Jesus went on to die and Peter was free to live.

In the dialogue between Peter and Jesus, the question "Do you love me?" was asked three times and the command "Feed my sheep" was given three times. This may be a parallel to the three denials of Jesus by Peter on the night of Jesus' betrayal. It is certain that the threefold command states Jesus' expectation of Peter in the clearest terms. There could be no remaining doubt concerning what Jesus wanted.

The command to feed the sheep is a definition of the kind of leadership Peter was to provide for the church. Jesus had already defined what it would mean to be a leader in 13:16. The one who was leader was to be servant of all. On the night of his betrayal Jesus had patterned the kind of leadership he intended for the church by washing the disciples' feet. On this occasion, his servanthood was demonstrated by cooking breakfast. He was Lord, but he served the meal. This was an example of what it meant to feed the sheep.

According to John, the sunrise breakfast is the final meal Jesus shared with his disciples. This meal repeated the truth Jesus had previously revealed at table. Table fellowship was a celebration of the power of self-giving love. Jesus had sat at table time and again with his disciples, with publicans and sinners, with people most persons sought to avoid, much less share a meal. All these meals had a cumulative effect. At last the disciples' eyes

Jesus' words are about mission. For us, as disciples today, what does it mean to feed Jesus' sheep? The text suggests we feed them on physical food, the Word, and relationships of intimacy. Ask: How do we do that in our congregation? If we take Jesus' words here as a commandment to us, what new ministries would we need to consider in our congregation?

were opened, and they were beginning to understand what table fellowship meant.

Jesus left table fellowship to give his life for his friends. Now he had returned in love to participate in table fellowship. He demonstrated his love for his friends by giving his life. This same self-giving love was manifested in the act of cooking their breakfast and serving them the meal. Finally, in the context of his self-giving love, Peter was commanded to be the shepherd of the sheep. Peter knew what it meant to be the shepherd because Jesus had already told him, "The good shepherd lays down his life for the sheep" (John 10:11). The good shepherd is like the perfect host who forfeits his life for his guest. At table, Jesus revealed a new way of living in relationship with one another in the world. The meal Jesus shared on the shore of Lake Galilee was life-giving and became life-transforming.

The power of Jesus' table fellowship is not only what he did during his earthly life, but what he continued to make possible in the lives of all who followed him. Tradition holds that, in obedience to Christ, Peter went to Rome and became the shepherd to the flock of Christ. Being the shepherd was not a position of honor but of service. In the church, the shepherd was the one who was the servant of all rather than the master of any. Peter knew that the shepherd was marked for slaughter by the Roman authorities who assumed that if they struck down the shepherd the sheep would be scattered. Peter appears to have been martyred, perhaps crucified, by Nero in A.D. 64. To the consternation of the Romans, his death, far from scattering the flock, became a new source of strength and courage. The Romans never understood what this meant. Killing the shepherd who is a servant never destroys the sheep.

The End ■

Since this session marks the end of this study, take a few minutes to reflect on what you've learned and to review actions the group has decided to take in response to the study. How will you work together to follow-through on those action decisions?

The truth found at the Table of the Lord is that no tyrant can ever defeat the power of self-giving love. Just as Jesus had rendered powerless the forces of sin and death in his exaltation upon the cross, souls nourished by his love continued in his love. As disciples, we continue to gather about Christ's table to celebrate the feast of the victory of our God. As long as we are one body fed and nourished by the one Bread, and as members of the one body serve one another, the mystery of God's eternal love lives in us, and we live in God.

Close With Prayer ■

God of revelation and reconciliation, thank you for all the new understandings we have gained in this study and for the ways in which we have drawn closer to you and to each other. Grant that, whenever we break bread, at the kitchen table, in the home of friends, or at the Lord's Table, we will remember you—and remember our brothers and sisters in need; in the name of the Christ. Amen.